BEAT YOUR BEST GOLF SCORE

TIPS AND ON-COURSE STRATEGY FROM TOP PGA TEACHING PROS

Edited by Tim Baker

BEAT YOUR BEST GOLF SCORE

TIPS AND ON-COURSE STRATEGY FROM TOP PGA TEACHING PROS

Edited by Tim Baker

A DAVID & CHARLES BOOK

David & Charles is an F+W Publications Inc. company
4700 East Galbraith Road
Cincinnati, OH 45236

First published in the UK in 2008
First published in the US in 2008

Today's Golfer

Source material courtesy of *Today's Golfer* magazine copyright © Emap Active
Photography by Bob Atkins and Angus Murray.

A catalogue record for this book is available from the British Library.

ISBN-13: 978-0-7153-2746-3 flexibound
ISBN-10: 0-7153-2746-1 flexibound

Printed in China by SNP Leefung
for David & Charles
Brunel House, Newton Abbot, Devon

Commissioning Editor: Neil Baber
Editor: Emily Pitcher
Desk Editor: Demelza Hookway
Project Editor: Joanna Chisholm
Assistant Designer: Joanna Ley
Production Controller: Kelly Smith

Visit our website at www.davidandcharles.co.uk

David & Charles books are available from all good bookshops; alternatively you can contact our Orderline on 0870 9908222 or write to us at FREEPOST EX2 110, D&C Direct, Newton Abbot, TQ12 4ZZ (no stamp required UK only); US customers call 800-289-0963 and Canadian customers call 800-840-5220.

CONTENTS

(cont.)

INTRODUCTION

Golf advice can be complicated and technical. What might be a revolutionary swing-thought to a low handicapper can simply confuse the beginner. A 100+ shooter is likely to be more interested in making clean contact with the ball than maintaining their spine angle throughout the swing! On the other hand, the advice to 'take your medicine' and play the percentages is not always what the expert golfer playing for birdies wants to hear.

Beat Your Best Golf Score is a collection of invaluable tips and advice tailored to your standard of play, whether you are trying to make it to double figures for the first time or to win the Club Championship. Part I offers a selection of technical tips, from driving to putting, that will help you to swing better and play improved shots. Part II then addresses your decision making on the course with a series of commonly encountered situations and alternative strategies for dealing with them.

Every golfer wants to keep improving and break through to the next level, but few of us will ever be able to achieve a swing like a pro or have the time to practise for hours a day. However, with the help of the advice in these pages you can set realistic goals, make the right decisions and maximize the chances of beating your best score.

PART I: TIPS ON TECHNIQUE

BUILD A PRE-SHOT ROUTINE

One of the most fundamental reasons high handicappers lack consistency is that they struggle to aim in the same direction for two shots in a row. One minute they are aiming at the rough on the left, the next it's the bunker on the right. Fortunately this is easy to fix.

There are two things that complicate lining up: first, the target is usually a long way away; and, second, you are standing side-on to it. But if you follow this six-step pre-shot routine you will address both these problems, as well as giving a regular pattern to your actions that has a great positive effect when it comes to making your overall game much more steady.

Step 1: Stand behind the ball-to-target line It's important you have a clear vision of the route your ball must take to reach its target – and you can picture this line best from behind the ball. Standing behind the line is also crucial to alignment. Look down your ball-to-target line to a few feet in front of the ball and find something on your line – a divot, a flower, an old tee peg…anything that won't move or blow away!

Step 2 : Pick your 'near' target On this shot there just happens to be a broken blue tee peg bang on your target line. Use this as a target reference. Square the clubface to this 'near' target, confident that it is also aiming at the far target.

Step 3: Introduce your back foot... Thanks to the blue tee, the clubface is aiming flush at the flag. The clubface can be used as a reference for your body alignment. Aim to build the feet, hips and shoulders square to the clubface. This is easiest to achieve in two stages. First, move your right or back foot into position.

Step 4: ...then your front Picture your toe line as square to the clubface aim. Double-check the face is still aiming at your 'near' target. Feel confident that your clubface and body alignment are going to hit the ball straight over your near target.

Step 5: Look back at the far target You've used a close-up target to align yourself. Now it's time to remind yourself of your ultimate target. Take one or two good looks at where you want the ball to end up. It's important to memorize your target – it helps you swing with purpose.

Step 6: Hit it! This system promotes a square aim, which helps you swing confidently through the ball. Repeat these six steps every time until they become second nature. Good aim is habit-forming, but it's an easy one to drift out of if you do not check it all the time.

HIGH HANDICAPPER

MID HANDICAPPER

GET YOUR SET-UP RIGHT

Few high handicappers set themselves up correctly at address. As a result, they give themselves little or no chance of hitting the ball well.

Here are five checks you should carry out before starting to swing the club. Get them all correct and you will see an immediate improvement in your scores.

Hands-on check Make sure at address that the back of the left hand and the right palm point at the target and the Vs formed on each hand by the index finger and thumb point between the chin and the right shoulder. Keep your grip pressure light.

Right palm points at the target…

…as does the back of the left hand

Aim at something near the ball and on the target line—like this leaf

Make it easy on yourself It's hardly rocket science to reveal that it is much easier to aim the clubhead accurately at something a few feet away than a target in the distance. So follow a tip from the great Jack Nicklaus and aim at something near you and on the target line, like a leaf, a discoloured area of grass or a divot.

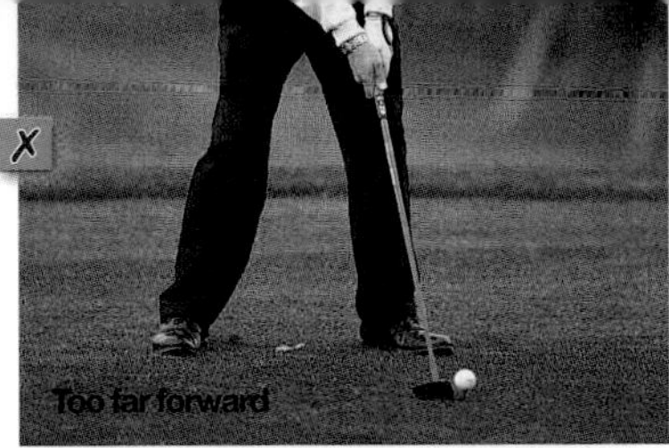

Positional strategy The position of the ball is crucial. With a driver, it should be opposite or just inside the front heel. Too far forward normally causes a pull to the left, and too far back a push out to the right. The ball comes back in the stance when you're playing irons.

Find the right line Feet, knees, hips and shoulders should all be aimed parallel to the target line. A club placed across them at address provides all the evidence you need to discover if you're on the right line.

Posture points Your posture should be athletic. Finding it is fairly simple – just flex your knees, bend slightly from the waist and then let your arms hang down naturally. There should be no tension in either your body or arms. When you grip your clubs from this position their soles should sit flat on the ground (the toes can be very slightly raised). If they don't, their lie is probably wrong for you and you should get your local PGA pro to check them out.

STAND THE CORRECT DISTANCE FROM THE BALL

For most high handicappers and novices, it's clear that many of their problems stem simply from the fact that they stand too near or too far from the ball at address.

There are a couple of dead-easy ways of finding the right distance (whatever club you're using) and how you should feel at address. I'll also describe what goes wrong when your set-up is awry.

Correct With the ball at the correct distance, your weight is mainly on the balls of the feet rather than the heels or toes. Your overall posture is tension-free, well-balanced and feels athletic, the chin is off the chest and the arms hang nicely relaxed from the shoulders.

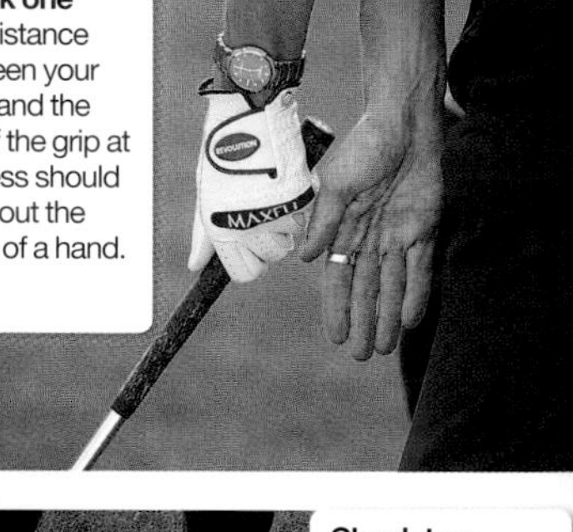

Check one
The distance between your thigh and the top of the grip at address should be about the width of a hand.

Check two
Lie a clubface down on the ground and place the ball a couple of inches inside the head. You can then find the correct distance by lining up the back of your heels with the butt end of the grip.

Too far Reaching at address will cause a flat swing path well inside the ball-to-target line. The player then lifts the arms in an attempt to get the club up, causing a change of spine angle. The result, again, is inconsistent ball-striking.

Too near Standing too near to the ball results in insufficient body turn (including the shoulders and hips), a lifting of the arms in the backswing and poor weight transfer. A multitude of faults can then occur, making consistent ball-striking virtually impossible.

HIGH HANDICAPPER

MID HANDICAPPER

DON'T LET YOUR FEET TRIP YOU UP

One of the many things that causes confusion with novices is how far apart the feet should be placed at address. And, even when told the width should be the same as the shoulders, many still fail to get it right. Even more experienced players don't realize that the root cause of some of their bad shots also stems from this fundamental error.

So let's begin by looking at what happens if your feet are too close together or too far apart.

Too close There is a lack of lower body stability and necessary resistance to the turning of the upper body, causing loss of balance and poor weight transference. The end result is an overall lack of power and control.

Too wide This stance prevents the body from making a full turn and the weight transferring to the front foot through the impact zone. The hands and arms take over, normally causing the ball to be hit to the left.

Getting it right Here is a very simple and effective way of finding the correct shoulder width for your feet at address. Place a club across your shoulders and measure the width between them **(below top)**. Put the club on the ground and mark the width with a couple of balls **(below centre)**. Place the inside of each heel against the balls **(bottom)**. Your feet are now the correct distance apart.

CHECK YOU'RE ON TARGET

It's amazing how few golfers, particularly high handicappers, aim their feet, hips and shoulders correctly at the target. They might think they do, but often they are miles out and usually to the left. Although the clubhead might be manipulated in the hands at address to point towards the target, the arms will nearly always swing the club along the line of the shoulders. Therefore it's imperative to set the shoulders (and the hips) parallel to the target line.

Here are three simple ways to check whether you are squaring yourself correctly to the target or are standing open (to the left) or closed (to the right). Two of the checks you can do yourself, while the third requires the assistance of a friend.

Check your aim with the club The simplest way to check where you are aiming (rather than where you think you are aiming) is to address the ball, retain your posture and then hold the club across your shoulders. You'll immediately see if you are aligned left **(above)**, right **(below left)** or square **(below right)**.

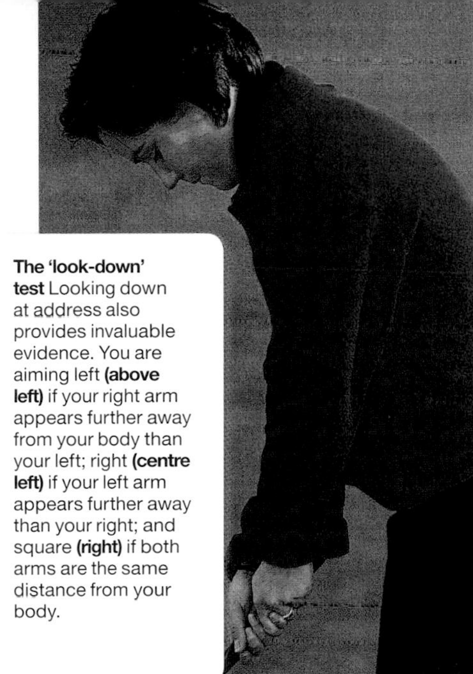

The 'look-down' test Looking down at address also provides invaluable evidence. You are aiming left **(above left)** if your right arm appears further away from your body than your left; right **(centre left)** if your left arm appears further away than your right; and square **(right)** if both arms are the same distance from your body.

Standing directly behind you, a friend will see nothing of your front forearm if you are aligned left of target. Virtually all of the inner part of the front arm will be visible if you are standing closed (aiming right of target). Only the top of the front forearm can be seen if you are aligned square to the target line.

SWING ON TRACK

Many golfers with swing problems are surprised to discover they have made a complete hash of things even before the club has reached halfway back. Once a sound set-up has been established, it is vital to take the club away from the ball correctly.

The clubhead, hands, arms, hips and chest should all turn away together so the chest is centred over the inner part of the right knee. The right leg remains in the same flexed position as it should be at address, and the spine angle is also unchanged. A club pointing away from the back foot will help you discover whether you are on the right track. When the club you're swinging is parallel to the ground it should be roughly in line with it.

Most high handicappers allow their hands and arms to dominate the takeaway and bring the clubhead too far inside the target line, usually leading to an out-to-in slicing path through impact.

Most high handicappers start their swing by dividing the clubhead too far inside the target line, leading to all sorts of problems and usually resulting in a slice **(above)**.

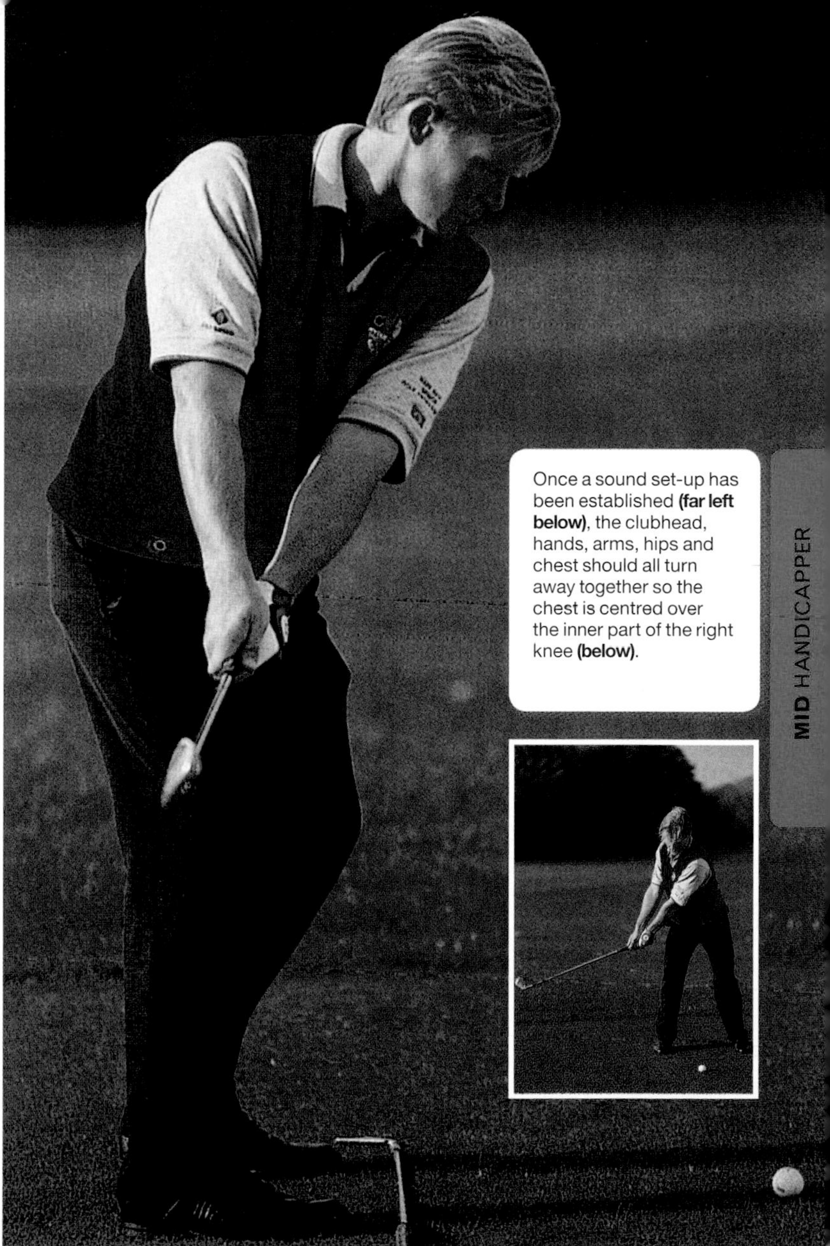

Once a sound set-up has been established **(far left below)**, the clubhead, hands, arms, hips and chest should all turn away together so the chest is centred over the inner part of the right knee **(below)**.

FEEL THE CORRECT IMPACT POSITION

If you have yet to break 100, it's a pretty safe bet that a few things are not quite as they should be when the clubhead connects with the ball at impact – the 'moment of truth'. If everything is correct, the clubface will come into the ball at good speed, square to the target line and at the right angle of attack.

But because it all happens so quickly, it is difficult for novices and high handicappers to know how everything should feel at this critical part of the swing. The best way is to find the correct impact position and then to take a restricted swing back and through the ball.

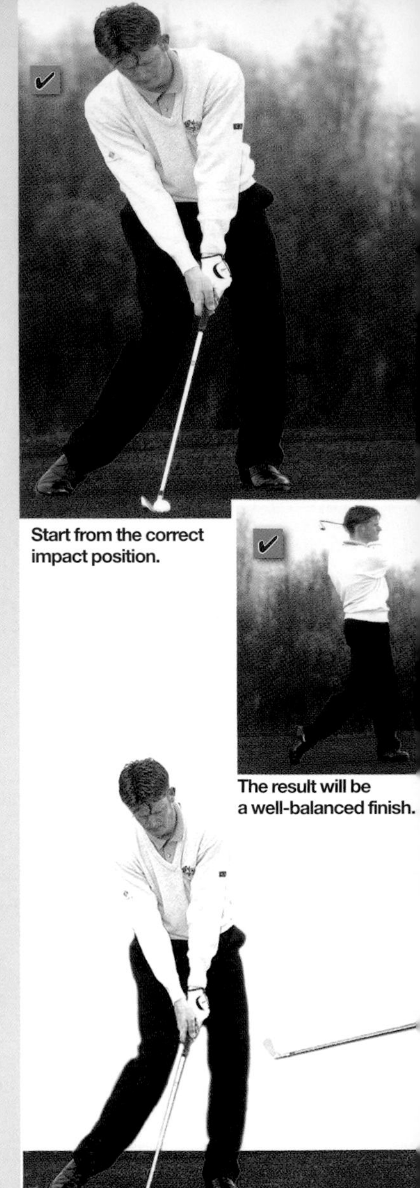

Start from the correct impact position.

The result will be a well-balanced finish.

Most poor scorers reach impact with their hands behind the ball…

…and finish looking like this.

Try this drill to achieve a perfect impact position. With your hands ahead of the clubhead, set the hips and knees about 20 degrees left of target and the shoulders square to the ball-to-target line. The right heel is off the ground, and the right knee is kicked in towards the ball **(below)**. The overall feeling is that your body weight is mainly on the left side.

Then just swing the club back and through the ball no further than waist height towards the target, feeling your weight transfer fully through and your body rotating. After a few swings, you will have a much clearer picture of how things should be.

STAY CONNECTED

'Ernie's swing looks really connected,' purr the golf pundits on TV. That's all very well, but what the blazes does it actually mean? Connection, a bit of a buzzword in golf, refers to the linking of the movement of body and arms during your swing. Ideally the two will move together and in harmony – your arms swinging while your body turns. This gives you your simplest action and the best chance of moving the club neatly up and down the line. But problems arrive in hordes when your body turn outpaces your arm swing, or vice versa.

So here's how to tie the two movements together. Logically enough, much of this is based around your shoulders – the link between body and arms. Work through these tips and see if they don't make your swing more coordinated and together.

Connection key #1
Left shoulder start

Left shoulder start

If you start everything in motion together, you've gone a long way to building a connected swing. To get instant feedback on how a connected takeaway should feel **(left above)**, hold the club in your left hand only and grip your left shoulder with your right hand (see far left stance). Start your backswing by pushing the club away from the ball with your left shoulder (see left stance). Feel your left shoulder move from the start of the swing, keeping its address relationship with your left arm and clubshaft. This stops your hands and arms moving ahead of your body and forces you to move as a unit. This all-together backswing will help you swing through this position, the clubshaft aiming pretty much down your target line when it's parallel to the ground **(left below)**.

Loads of hackers have the thought of left shoulder under chin **(above)**. Don't. It's a bad target to have. It leads to a stilted and short shoulder turn as your shoulders try to rotate on too upright an angle. Your shoulders stop moving while your arms try to carry on to the top. Result? A disjointed movement and loss of connection.

Instead, feel your left shoulder brush past your chin **(left)**. This thought keeps your left shoulder up on the way back, which gives your swing room and helps you create leverage on the way down. It also allows your shoulders to turn more fully and retain their relationship with your swinging arms.

LET YOUR POSTURE MAKE YOUR SWING PATH CONSISTENT

MID HANDICAPPER

Many golfers fail to shoot in the 80s because of an inconsistent swing path. That is, they swing across the ball, from in-to-out or more usually out-to-in, which, with an open face, leads to a slice. But few players realize the root cause of this off-line swing path: faulty posture. The ball is on the ground so you must bend over the right amount to hit it. But if your spine angle is too bent or upright you can't swing back and through on a uniform, down-the-line plane. So what is the right amount? Here's how to set your spine angle through the bag and a drill to keep it spot-on.

Set your posture Run through this two-step plan to build the right posture and spine angle with every club in the bag.

- Take up your normal grip.
- Stand upright with the club out in front of you **(above)**, shaft level with the ground. Keep your back straight.
- Flex your knees until they are over your laces.

- Keeping your back straight, bend over smoothly from your hips until the clubhead rests on the turf **(above)**.
- Do not alter the relationship between arms and body. Your upper arms should stay close to your chest.
- Keep the angle between your arms and clubshaft the same.

Maintain your posture Setting the right spine angle is one thing, but it can only improve your swing path if you hold on to that spine angle as you turn back and through. Focus on the midway points of your backswing and through-swings to check this.

Driver The typical driver is 45 inches long and is the longest club in your bag. When you run through the two-step drill to set your spine angle, the longer shaft means the clubhead hits the ground sooner. That means you don't have to bend over quite so much. With your driver, your spine angle should be a little more upright.

Feel your backswing rotate around your spine **(top inset)**. Avoid straightening up. As you swing through, maintain your spine angle until after the club has passed hip height **(bottom inset)**. The swing momentum will pull you more upright.

9-iron At 36 inches, the 9-iron is nearly a foot shorter than your driver. When it comes to setting your address spine angle, you must bend over further from your hips to get the clubhead to sit on the turf. Again, during your backswing your aim is to keep this spine angle intact **(top inset)**. Achieve this happy habit and you'll go a long way to making an on-line backswing every time. Once more, hold on to that angle until after the club swings forward past your hips **(bottom inset)**. Your swing will feel more upright with the 9-iron – that's fine and natural. The plane of swing is dictated by your spine angle.

WATCH OUT FOR LOCK KNEE

One of the most common faults of mid and high handicappers is the straightening and locking of the right knee during the backswing and at the top of the swing. In addition to leading to a poor turn and lack of power, a locked knee also usually causes a very flat swing around the body and an over-the-top action to get back into the ball...and a big slice.

A powerful coiling action and correct swing path – resulting in long and straight shots – can only be achieved if you maintain the degree of flex in the right knee at address throughout the swing and you ensure that the weight remains on the inside of your right foot.

Nicely on line at the top...

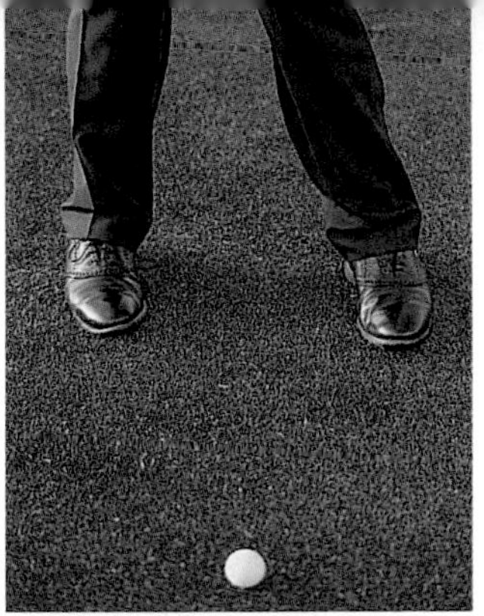

The drill One of the best drills to achieve the desired action is to point the right foot inwards at address and keep it there to the finish **(left)**. You will soon feel the required pressure on the knee and appreciate the sensation of a powerful coiling action between the lower and upper body – and, of course, hit some nice solid shots.

HIGH HANDICAPPER

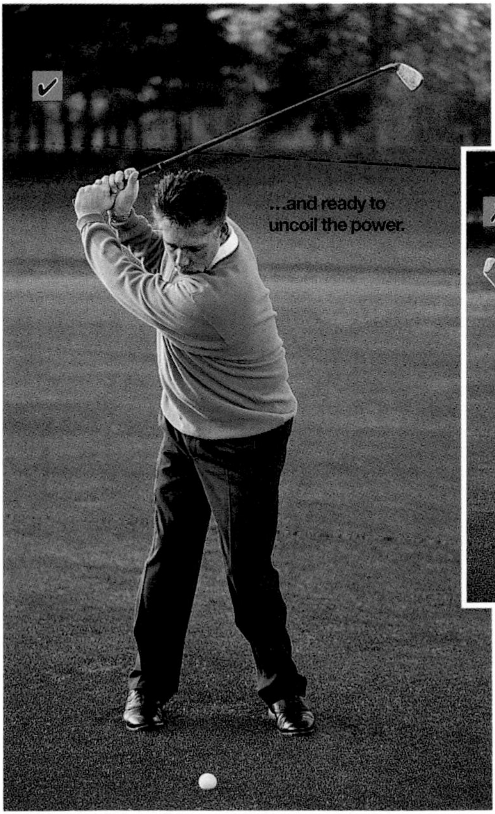
✓
...and ready to
uncoil the power.

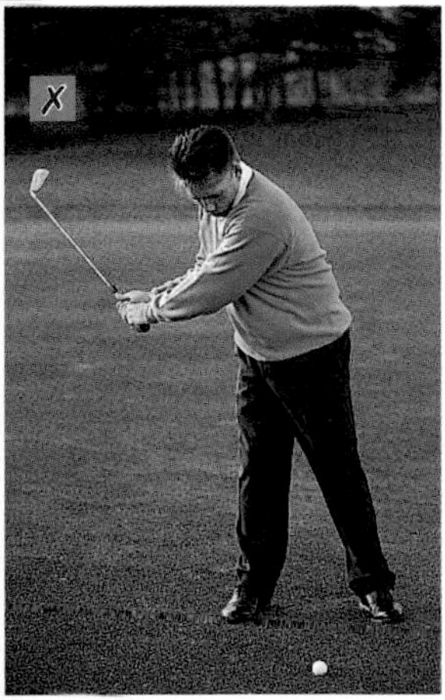
✗

MID HANDICAPPER

SET-UP FOR A PURE STRIKE

A survey was taken recently of the set-ups of the world's top 70 tour pros. It indicated that, when it came to ball-striking, there were three key elements they all adjusted to maximize their effectiveness from driver to wedge. Those key elements related to the spine angle, the feet and the hands. Here's how you can take a leaf out of the pros' book and improve your ball-striking no end by tightening your set-up.

WOODS

Pro secret 1: Backward lean Watch the top players and you will see they lean away from the target with their bodies at set-up **(right above)**. For right-handers it causes the left shoulder to rise and the right shoulder to drop. This gives them two key advantages:

- It promotes a big gap between left shoulder and knee at the top **(right below)**. The bigger this gap is, the more coil and power you will generate.
- Dropping the right shoulder helps settle a little extra weight into the back foot. It's important to shift your weight back behind the ball on the backswing, and this set-up move gives you a headstart.

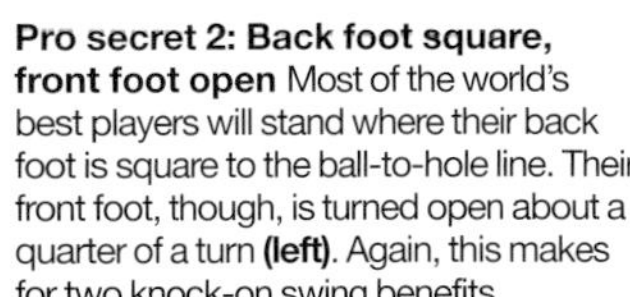

Pro secret 2: Back foot square, front foot open Most of the world's best players will stand where their back foot is square to the ball-to-hole line. Their front foot, though, is turned open about a quarter of a turn **(left)**. Again, this makes for two knock-on swing benefits.

- The open front foot helps you clear your front side (left for right-handers) as you swing forward, giving your arms room to swing through **(below centre)**. This is vital to good ball-striking because if your body blocks your arm swing you'll be forced to flick at the ball with your hands.
- The square back foot helps firm up your back knee and hip. This helps your right side resist the coiling in your backswing, building powerful torque.

Pro secret 3: Top knuckle level with back of ball This hand position effectively puts the hands 'behind' the clubhead, as you can see by the slight backward lean in the clubshaft **(left)**. This adds a little loft to the face and, by keeping the golfer's midriff behind the ball, prepares the player for an ideal driver strike.

- Hands-behind-ball will help you make the perfect sweeping action through impact **(above right)**. You will catch the ball just on the upward swing, helping you hit the ball on a high, hanging trajectory.

IRONS

Pro secret 1: Spine is straighter Although the right shoulder is still a little lower than the left **(right)**, this is more to do with the right hand being under the left on the grip than any spine lean. As the irons get shorter, the spine gets more vertical (as seen from face-on).

Pro secret 2: Hands ahead For the wedge, you will see most pros now have the back of their lower hand ahead of the front of the ball (ball position generally moves back from left instep to centre of stance).

.

A straighter spine is going to encourage more of a downward hit on the ball.

Hands are now ahead of the ball, again encouraging a descending blow and backspin.

Feet stay the same as for the woods. You still need to clear your left side with irons.

Pro secret 3: Feet constant One thing that has no need to change is the stance. Whatever the club, you still need resistance on the way back and clearance on the way through. These measures promote a crisp downward strike, helping the golfer pinch the ball between clubface and turf and producing packs of backspin.

PICTURE THE BALL FOR THE RIGHT STRIKE

If you want to improve your ball-striking you must first understand how your clubs are designed to work. Because the lofts on the clubface change through the bag, how you attack the ball must change too. The low-lofted 3-wood needs a different approach to help the ball up into the air than the wedge, whose face has masses of loft. To start off, avoid getting too technical – simply picturing how you would hit different-sized balls will help you create the right angle of attack into the ball for each club.

3-wood

Your 3-wood is built for distance and has little loft on the clubface (on average about 15 degrees). This means you need a sweeping angle of attack to help the ball up into the air. Imagine you are about to hit a football over a hedge with a golf club. How would you do it? The only possible way is to position the ball opposite your front foot (the one closer to the hole) and try to sweep it up into the air.

Make the same sweep **(inset)** with a 3-wood. The fact the ball is teed up will help you. Make sure you keep your head and body behind the ball as you swing through impact.

Your wedge is built for height and accuracy (52 degrees loft on the face). Getting the ball up is not a problem. Your priority now is to make a clean strike. This time imagine how you'd hit a marble into the air. With such a small ball on the ground, there's no way you'll sweep it up: instead hit down, stunning it up like you'd hit down on water to make a splash. Do this with your wedge play **(inset)**. Feel the ball is back to the centre of your stance, with your head and body ahead. These two measures will help you make the downward strike you need to send the ball up.

The face of your 5-iron – the longest iron you need to be using at the moment – has around 28 degrees loft. The ideal approach falls right between the sweeping, slightly upward strike you need from your 3-wood and the downward, stunning technique that best suits your wedge. This time, picture how you would use your 5-iron to strike a tennis ball. Picturing the tennis ball is ideal for the level strike needed for mid-irons, and lofted fairway woods. Position the ball midway between your left heel and stance centre **(inset)**. Aim to keep head and body in front of the ball at impact.

SWING IN BALANCE FOR A BETTER STRIKE

Balance is crucial to control and, therefore, good ball-striking. Many golfers think the best way to stay balanced through the swing is by keeping their head still. In fact it is the opposite. In a well-balanced swing, your weight must shift gently with the momentum of the swinging club – back on the backswing and forward on the way through – and your head must move in harmony with that subtle weight shift. Avoid these three errors to improve your balance.

Balance error 1: Weight back in your heels In bending down to the ball, many golfers overbend their knees. This can force their weight back into the heels. As well as giving you limited mobility, it means you are off-balance before you've even started the club back. Recognize this **(inset)**? Weight in heels tend to promote a very flat backswing, the club immediately sailing round behind your back. From this overly 'inside' position the golfer will be forced to loop the club up and over at the top, swinging down from out-to-in. Look out for a slice.

Solution to error 1: Weight through the middle Lean forward until you feel your weight running through the balls of your feet. This puts you in a well-balanced position to start your swing. Moving your weight forward encourages a more on-line backswing **(inset)**. You will swing through this correct position – butt of the club pointing at or near your target line – when your weight runs through the middle of your feet.

Balance error 2: Head stays still going back If you try to keep your head still as you swing the club back, you will prevent your weight moving with the swinging club **(far left)**. This puts your weight at odds with your swing. You will make a stilted, awkward backswing and feel powerless at the top.

Solution to error 2: Move by half a head Instead, allow your head to move gently to your right (right-handers), away from the target. It can help you to picture where your nose is at address. Then feel your head move half a head laterally away from your target through the backswing so that at the top your left ear is where your nose was at set-up **(left)**. Your head is heavy; it doesn't need to move a long way to guarantee your weight moves behind the ball.

Balance error 3: Head still on downswing Any misguided effort to keep your head still on the way through will again set your weight at odds with the swinging club **(right)**. Look to build forward momentum on the through-swing, weight moving to your front foot.

Solution to error 3: Head moves forwards Instead, as you swing through the ball allow your head to move laterally towards the target. Make sure you finish with weight on your front foot **(far right)**.

Try this balance drill Place a clubshaft under your armpits and grip it as shown **(left)**. With your torso make a backswing turn until the butt of the club points at your back toe. Now make a through-swing. Keep rotating until the head of the club points at your left toe. This will help you feel how your weight should move during the swing.

DEAL WITH THE PRESSURE ON THE TEE

Take a look at the picture on the far right. What grabs your attention? Is it the distant town of Quarteira? Is it the pin? Or is it that humungous orange abyss munching into the left side of the hole? Trouble – deep trouble – is often eyecatching and seizes your attention. Like the snake in *Jungle Book*, once you start looking at it, it can mesmerize you and send you on your way to oblivion. Even if it's in a 'blimey, wouldn't want to go down there' kind of way, you still see yourself playing the very shot you want to avoid. And once you start picturing it, you are much more likely to perform it.

So your first step is to gain control of what you look at as you survey the shot. But even then, fear and pressure will keep attacking you. Follow this routine and you will play these shots with far more confidence and with much better results.

'Record' your success Draw on a memory of a previous successful shot. Remember a good shot by assigning a special movement to 'tag' it – maybe twirling the club in the fingers **(above)**, a tagging device used by top pros. In this way you can build up a library of good memories to recall in pressure situations.

Start low, start smooth The golf swing is a chain reaction; if you can begin your swing with poise and control you will set the pattern for your entire action. Keep your first move away from the ball under control by monitoring the pace – quick and jerky spells trouble. Make this smooth start your only swing-thought **(above)**. It's vital your attention is locked on to your target safe-zone throughout the shot. Too many swing-thoughts and you'll forget what you are trying to achieve.

Where to land? Before you even think about selecting a club, pick a safe landing spot for your ball. This spot must be surrounded by an area big enough to give you confidence that, even if you miss it, your ball winds up in a playable position. This could mean playing away from the green. An achievable target helps you make a committed and confident golf swing – vital if you are to stay out of trouble. Once you've given yourself a manageable target to play to, picture the way the ball would fly to land there. Finally, visualize the swing.

Pick more than enough club If you pick your usual club for the distance, you place added pressure on your shoulders by feeling you need to strike the ball perfectly to catch your safe target area. By taking a club more than normal (e.g. a 5-iron instead of 6) you allow yourself to feel that you'll end up safe even with a slight mishit.

Seeing a stronger club in your hands also tells you there is no need to swing at your limit. It allows you to make a controlled swing – crucial when you're under pressure.

Breathe easy Anxiety makes your breathing shallow and quick. That's great if you need to perform some kind of explosive action, like running away or fighting an attacker. But golf needs serenity and calmness. You will find these easier to achieve by slowing down your breathing. Do this by focusing on your stomach. See how fat you can make yourself by breathing in, then release your breath slowly.

DITCH THE WRONG ADVICE TO GAIN POWER

Most learner golfers are bombarded with apparently handy hints from the off. And one of the trickiest things about trying to improve is knowing which of those tips will help you and which will do more harm than good. Unfortunately, when it comes to power, many 'words of wisdom' fall into this latter camp; 'keep your head still', 'control the club', even something as simple as 'turn' can make your action as limp as a soggy biscuit. So here are three power-draining pieces of advice to avoid. Work on each one in turn and add some snap to your action.

Power point 1: Get your grip right A good grip is essential. The problem is that the club seems most under control when you hold it in your palms. But this is no good for power. Try throwing two balls down the fairway. Hold the first ball in your palm **(inset)**. You will find you can't throw it very far as your palm grip immobilizes your wrist.

Solution to point 1 Throw a second ball, held in your fingers. Now your wrist has the freedom to hinge back and forward **(inset)**, adding a forceful whip to your throw. Hold the club in your fingers, especially with your top hand. Now your wrist hinge is a lever that will add distance to your shots.

Power point 2: Head movement The phrase 'keep your head still' is used too often. The logic is that a still bonce will help you strike the ball accurately. In any power move you must use your weight. In golf this means moving on to your back foot as you swing back, then driving powerfully on to your front foot through the ball. But a still head works against this weight shift. Try it and you'll be in this weak position, weight centred or falling forward on to your front foot.

Solution to point 2 Allow your head to move back as you swing back. Feel your weight move into your right side (right-handers) – over your back knee is not a bad thought. Only from here can you drive forward with real intent to smack the ball.

Power point 3: Power turn Common advice is to turn the club on an inside path at the start of the swing. It's easy to overdo this and whip the clubhead back past your back heel, producing a cramped and powerless position. The swing loses coordination and therefore power as the rotating body dominates your arm swing. The clubhead gets 'trapped' behind your body. It tends to lead to a loopy over-the-top action and a slice.

Solution to point 3 Feel the club is in front of your turning body as you take the club back. It gives you these benefits:

- Better coordination between arm swing and body turn.
- An on-line takeaway aiding a downswing that hits straight down the line.

GET YOUR POSTURE RIGHT FOR REAL POWER

The world's top players hit the ball enormous distances, and apparently with minimum effort. It's a joy to watch, but also frustrating. When amateurs try for the same, easy swing they usually cannot generate similar effortless power. To discover how the best do it, you need to consider body angles and posture. That's because it is through posture that your body can build a taut, coiled backswing that promotes a speedy unwind coming down and gives the top player that deceptive power. So here's how to build the correct body angles into your set-up.

Power-LESS set-up This hunched position is sloppy and unathletic **(below)**. The bent back makes it much harder to achieve a good rotational movement. This position **(inset)** is about as good as you could hope from the hunched set-up. You can create no torque, and no power for the downswing.

Power-FULL set-up The first thing to notice is the straight spine. As well as allowing a fuller backswing, this back position is less likely to cause injury. Also note the small curve in the small of the back, just as when standing upright. Now with back straight, the complete backswing **(inset)** winds the upper body powerfully against the stable lower half.

Stand with your spine upright and clubhead at shoulder height. Try to swing the clubhead in a perfect circle round your shoulders.

Try the circle drill Your most powerful action means swinging the club on a full, wide, almost circular arc around your body. But it's not easy to find this width when bent over the ball. So here **(left top, left centre and below)** is a circle drill that will help you apply the arc from that upright swing to your normal address position.

Keeping your back straight, bend over until the clubhead is knee height. Make the same swing as before, again feeling the club is drawing that perfect circle.

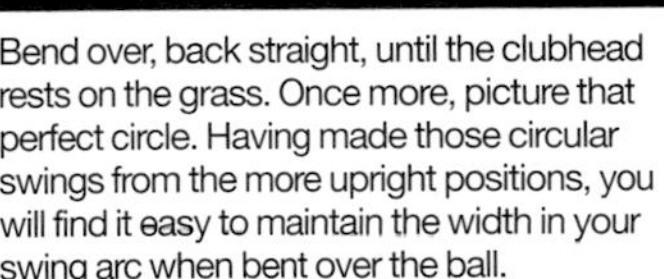

Bend over, back straight, until the clubhead rests on the grass. Once more, picture that perfect circle. Having made those circular swings from the more upright positions, you will find it easy to maintain the width in your swing arc when bent over the ball.

HIGH HANDICAPPER

MID HANDICAPPER

HIT IT UNDER THE WIND

Most high and mid handicappers hit the ball with slice spin. Therefore, if their shot pattern is combined with a left-to-right wind, you can put money on their shots being blown into trouble on the right from the tee. Here, without having to make complicated swing changes, are three things you can do at set-up to help put the ball on the fairway.

In order to keep the ball under the wind, tee it a little lower than normal to help promote a more penetrating flight. Then concentrate on making a nice, smooth swing.

LOW TEE NORMAL TEE

Tee the ball as far right on the teeing ground as possible so that you can hit it into the wind and reduce the left-to-right effect.

WIND DIRECTION

Ensure you can see at least three knuckles of the left hand when you look down at address. This will result in the face of the club being a little closed at impact **(inset)** to keep the ball left and low.

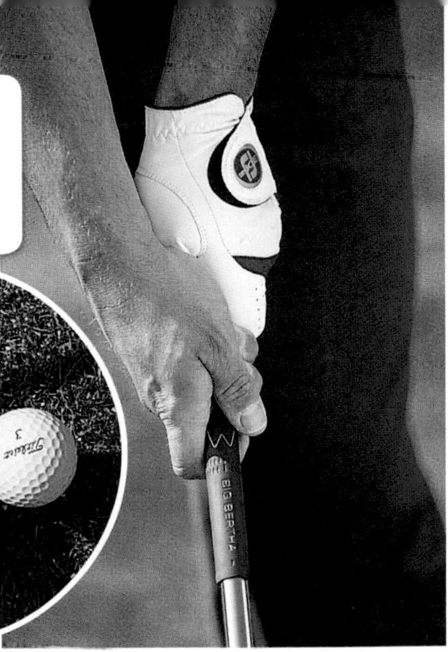

USE YOUR LOWER HALF TO ADD YARDS

It's tempting to see power as an upper-body-dominated affair, bulging biceps and rippling shoulders clobbering the ball into submission. And yes, you can hit hard with your upper body. But power is no use without control, and this is where your lower half comes in. Good lower-body technique provides a base for you to hit from. It channels and enhances your power. It's the difference between throwing a ball when stood on dry land or throwing one from a swamp. Here are five steps to using your lower half to control and boost your power.

Step 1: Knees wide at set-up As you address the ball, bow your knees out a little so the caps face away from each other – a touch outward of straight ahead (below). This helps build torque – that powerful winding of the upper body against resistance from your lower half. Angling your knees away from each other pre-sets that resisting feeling and gives you the sensation of strength and athleticism.

Step 2: Knees over shoelaces Look no further than this reference point when it comes to how much you should flex your knees **(right)**. If you flex any more than this you overactivate your leg muscles, making your legs tense and static.

Step 3: Weight into inside of back foot at the top Your weight should be on your back foot as the backswing ends **(right below)**. But be more specific than that – feel it running down the length of the inside of the foot. This will help you resist rotating your upper body, giving you a braced feeling as you complete your coil. It also gives you something to push off from to start your downswing.

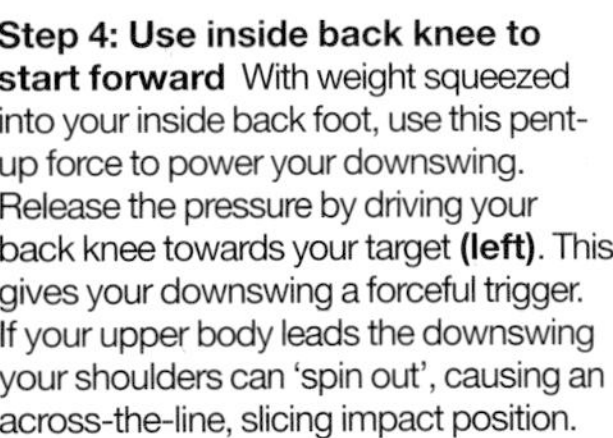

Step 4: Use inside back knee to start forward With weight squeezed into your inside back foot, use this pent-up force to power your downswing. Release the pressure by driving your back knee towards your target **(left)**. This gives your downswing a forceful trigger. If your upper body leads the downswing your shoulders can 'spin out', causing an across-the-line, slicing impact position.

Step 5: Finish with front leg strong As you head in to impact, practise feeling your front knee snap back into its socket, putting your leg into a straight and strong position **(inset)**. You must let your arms swing freely through the ball. If your back knee is flexed your body stays in the way, slowing the clubhead.

SLIDE IT AWAY FROM TROUBLE

Hazards down the left side of a hole usually present problems for better players because their 'bad' shot is normally a draw or hook.

When faced with this situation, keep things simple by making a couple of changes on the tee to produce what might be called 'the slider', because it slides the ball to the right and away from the trouble.

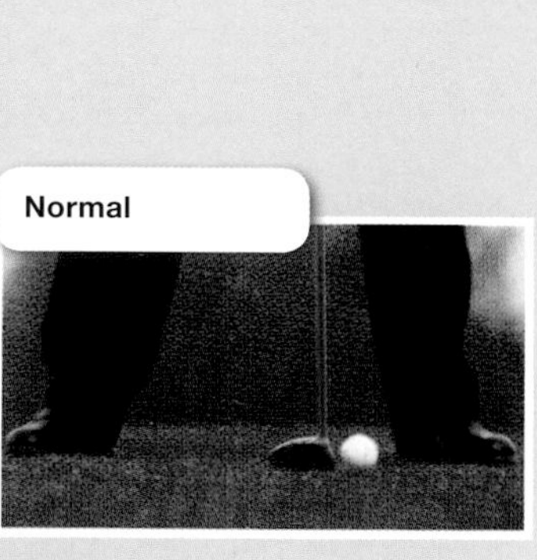

Normal

Move the ball about three inches further back than normal and lean a little to the left **(right below)**, with the hands ahead of the ball and weight slightly favouring the front foot **(right)**. These changes combine to keep ahead of the ball to produce a steeper angle of attack and make it virtually impossible to release the clubhead fully through impact, keeping the clubface open when it meets the ball.

The slider

The slider

REGULATE YOUR FORCE TO CONTROL DISTANCE

As your game improves, the margins between your good and bad shots get smaller. But one area where lower handicappers often struggle is adjusting the distance they hit the ball. Tour players hit the ball pin-high at will, and it isn't all about caddies and yardages – it's also about being able to apply the required force to the ball.

The pros have two keys for this. First, they have reference points for controlling backswing length; and, second, they have another set of references for controlling how hard they hit the ball. Use these references to boost your own power control.

Make your backswing six inches long! Control the length of your backswing and you take a big step to controlling distance. Many golfers struggle to do this because their reference point for backswing length is the clubshaft: is it parallel? past parallel? short? But you can't really see where it is, and you can manipulate the position easily through wrist hinge. Instead, focus on your left or forward shoulder. Make yourself aware of its position at set-up.

Stay aware of your left shoulder as you make your backswing. A full turn will see it make a six-inch journey from its starting position to under your chin. This small move is easier to see, feel and regulate; it also guarantees a full body wind, a much truer measure of backswing length.

Use the 1–5 system to regulate your force A common cause of poor distance control is irregular swing speed. Changes here lead to timing discrepancies that can make the difference between hitting the green or finding the trap in front of it. But you will only regulate swing speed when you have some parameters to measure it. Use a 1–5 system for this.

One on your scale means swinging about as slowly as you can. Make a couple of swings to establish your mark-one pace.

Five on your scale means swinging as fast as you can without losing balance. Ignore where the ball goes.

Three on your scale means splitting the difference. This represents your ideal swing speed; you have now given it a value.

LEARN TO HIT HIGH AND LOW

Although it is unrealistic to expect high handicappers to fade or draw the ball to order, they really need to have a basic knowledge of how to control the height of their shots... particularly when playing courses with plenty of trees about.

But don't panic – most of the work in achieving success with these shots is in the way you set up to the ball rather than complicated swing techniques. This is how it's done.

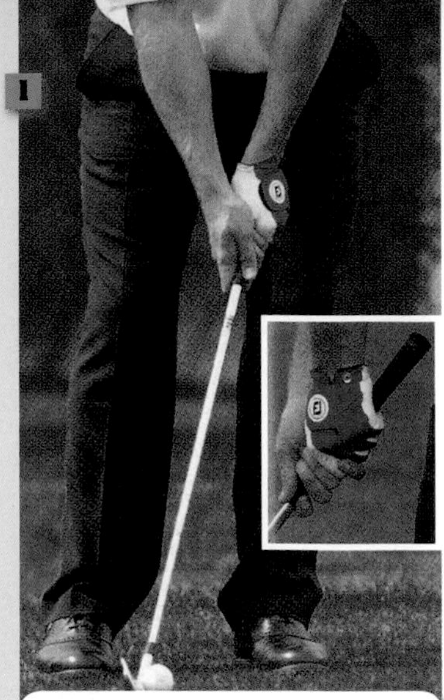

PUNCH IT LOW

The set-up With hands placed down the grip, the ball is positioned just to the right of centre and weight favours the front leg. The hands are ahead of the ball, and the loft of the club (a 6-iron) has been naturally decreased.

HITTING IT HIGH

The set-up This particular shot calls for the most lofted club in the bag – in most cases, a sand iron. To further ensure a high flight, the ball is positioned forward of centre and the weight slightly favours the right leg. The feet, hips and shoulders are all aligned a little left of the target line and the clubface a little right (known as open).

PUNCH IT LOW
Backswing
Because of the set-up, the backswing is automatically steeper and shorter than normal. From here, all you have to do is to hit steeply down for a ball-then-turf impact to punch the ball out powerfully and low.

PUNCH IT LOW
The finish Don't worry that the through-swing is curtailed – this is a natural result of the steep and accelerating downward path into the ball that the set-up generates.

HITTING IT HIGH
Top of swing The adjustments made at address are sufficient for the ball to fly high, so all you need to do is swing as normal to the top.

HITTING IT HIGH
Impact and finish Have faith in the additional loft you have already created. As you slide the club under the ball, try to keep the sole as low to the ground as possible after the strike. This will eliminate the temptation to scoop or flick at the ball.

CHOOSE THE RIGHT CLUB

Mid handicappers frequently lose shots to par simply because of poor club selection – one of the biggest dilemmas being whether to use an iron or fairway wood for certain shots. Here are three typical examples and the club you should use for each.

Semi rough The size and design of its head and its playability makes the fairway wood the choice here. Because the normal sweeping motion would cause a thinned shot, the ball needs to be positioned a couple of inches further back in the stance than normal to create a slightly steeper angle of attack.

Poor lie on fairway Don't even think about your woods when the ball is sitting down in the fairway, particularly if there's a hint that it's come to rest in an old shallow divot **(below)**. Take a more lofted iron than you would normally use for the distance and – by positioning the ball back in the stance and concentrating a little more weight on the left foot – hit it sharply down **(right)**.

On top of rough Because an iron could easily pass right under the ball with hardly any contact, this is most definitely another job for the wood. Be extremely careful here not to ground the club fully, as the ball will probably move and land you with a one-stroke penalty. Hovering the sole just above the grass also reduces any risk of snagging on the takeaway.

BE REALISTIC IN THE ROUGH

You're about 150 yards from the green and the ball is sitting in thick rough. So you ask yourself what club will get you to the green. Wrong! As someone who has yet to break 100, what you should be asking is which club will virtually guarantee that your next shot is from the fairway rather than another from the rough. In other words, you're looking for damage limitation...and realism. In this case, it's a job for the pitching wedge.

1

The thick grass 'grabs' the neck of the club **(above)** and forces it to close (point left) and become delofted at impact. To counteract this, turn the hands a little to the left when you take your grip so that it opens the clubface to point right of target when you address the ball.

2

Grip down the handle **(above)** and a fraction tighter than normal for extra control in the rough.

To produce a steep swing and avoid being tangled up in the thick grass, also make sure the ball is back in your stance (midway between centre and the back foot) and your weight favours the left side **(left)**.

Now, with your body aimed a little right of target **(below left)**, make your normal swing and, to ensure acceleration through impact, concentrate on trying to achieve a full followthrough **(below right)**. The ball will fly to the fairway.

WORK ON YOUR TEMPO TO CONTROL BACKSPIN

When you take up the game and need to build confidence in striking your chip shots, it's only logical that you learn a ball-back, hands-forward technique that allows you to hit down on the ball. But once your skill levels rise you will notice a drawback with this method – the ball squeezes out low and fast and without a huge amount of control. So now that you are a potential 70-shooter it's time to rethink this technique so that you produce a more forward-hitting motion. If your basic swing-thought is to hit the ball forward, not down, it opens up a whole range of shot options for you. Here's how to do it.

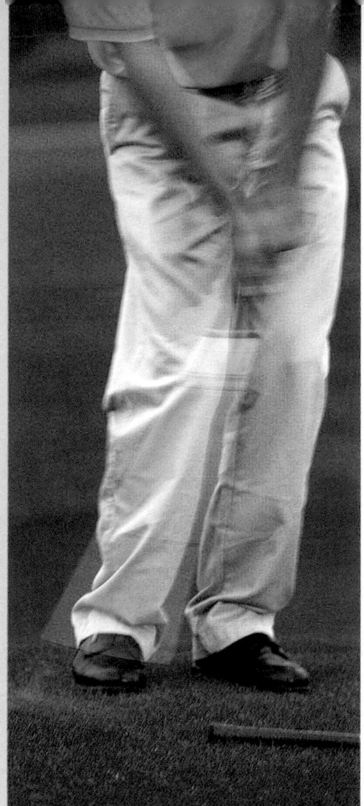

Step 1: Hit the grip One of the best ways to get the feel of hitting forward and not down is by striking a rubber golf grip (you can get one cheaply from your club pro). Simply place it on the ground, pointing it at your target. Picture the angle of attack you would need to make in order to hit the grip any distance forward. You should be imagining a forward hit – anything downward and the club will bounce up off the grip. Go ahead and hit the grip with perhaps a half-swing. Experiment with a few shots. Which angle of attack knocks the grip furthest? That's the one you should use.

Step 2: Change ball position Your old, ball-back ball position makes it hard to hit the ball forward **(below)**. A ball placed back of centre encourages a chopping action down on the ball.

Instead play the ball opposite the middle of your chest. Dangle a club from your sternum to help you picture where that should be.

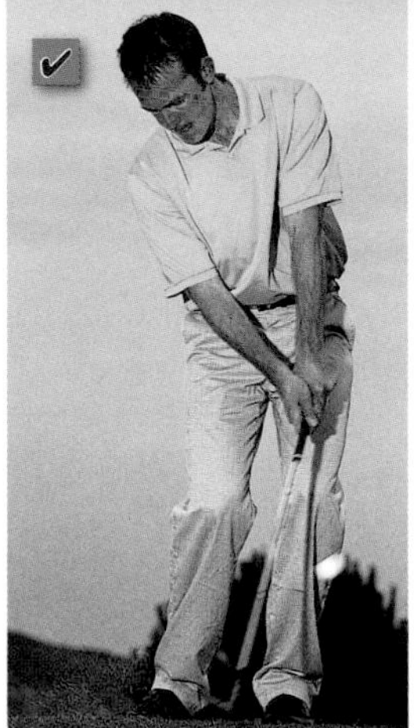

This new ball position will feel forward (closer to the hole) of your old one and encourages impact with the clubhead's arc levelled out.

Step 3: Clubhead outside hands – back and through This technique works best with your hands 'quiet' through the action **(above left)**. Don't allow your hands and wrists to work the clubhead back 'inside' the line of your hands. Picture the clubface staying on the ball-to-hole line throughout the move **(above right)**. It won't – it'll still work inside back and through as your body turns – but as an intention it will help keep your hands passive.

Step 4: 'Scrape the clubface through the grass' This is another good thought to promote a level hit. Try to let the bottom of the club graze the grass for as long as possible through the impact zone.

KEEP IT SIMPLE TO PITCH IT CLOSE

MID HANDICAPPER

The pitch shot from about 90 yards and in seems to present more than its fair share of problems to the average golfer, often resulting in clubhead deceleration through the hitting area and a hopelessly weak shot. Here's how it should be played.

1

The set-up With the ball positioned in the middle of the stance, let your weight favour the front foot and grip the club fairly lightly. The front foot should be drawn back a few inches from the parallel ball-to-target line, and the toes splayed out a few degrees towards the target. The overall set-up is tension-free.

2

The swing The position of the feet will automatically restrict the swing to about three-quarters of its normal length. From here, just concentrate on accelerating the clubhead through the hitting area and turning the shoulders and body so that the chest faces the target in the followthrough. Don't make the mistake of trying to create clubhead speed on the way down solely with the wrists and hands.

BE AGGRESSIVE WITH A SHORT PITCH

The 60- to 80-yard pitch shot with a sand or pitching wedge is a difficult one for most amateurs because they fail to grasp the fact that, although not usually a full shot, it has to be played with plenty of aggression. Any hint of clubhead deceleration or helping the ball into the air will result in exactly the opposite of what you are trying to achieve – a controlled shot with plenty of bite to keep the ball on the green and near the pin.

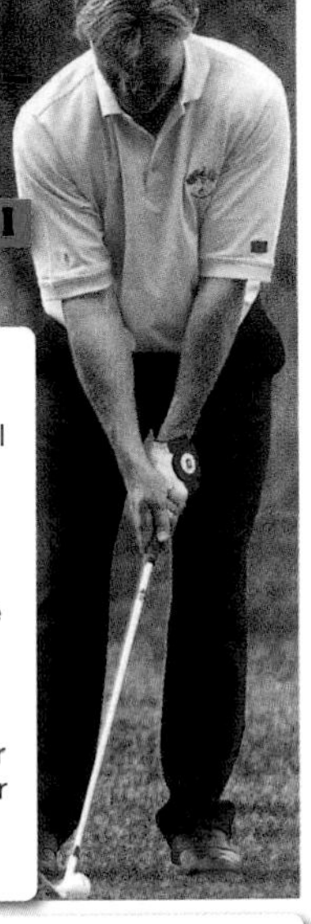

1

The set-up Adopt a more narrow stance than normal and position the ball midway between centre and the back foot, ensuring it is to the right of the head and hands. Grip halfway down the handle and let your body weight favour the left side.

2

At the top The backswing calls for plenty of wrist cock to guarantee a steep angle of attack into the ball. Exactly how far back you take the club obviously depends on which of the two clubs you are using and the exact distance to be covered.

3

Impact and through An aggressive steep swing into the ball results in a ball-then-turf contact, a big divot and plenty of check on the ball when it lands.

AVOID THE DUFF CHIP

The biggest problem the 100-shooter faces with chips is getting the clubface on the back of the ball cleanly. The trouble here is that the club is travelling so slowly that any contact with ground before ball causes the club to stall and the ball to move as if covered in superglue. Duffs come from two significant faults.

First is a poor angle of attack. High handicappers must build an action that hits down on the ball to give them the feeling they will not hit the ground first. A change of set-up can help you here. Second is rhythm. So many players swing back too far and then slow down into the ball to avoid hitting it too far. Again, this leads to a heavy strike. These lessons can help tackle both faults.

Rule 1: Mimic impact at address Find an impact position in which you are making a descending blow on to the back of the ball, almost as if you were trying to drive the ball into the ground. The loft on the clubface still makes the ball rise. This has two big benefits:

- Hands lead the clubface into the ball.
- Weight is mainly on your left (or forward) side.

Build the following into your address position. Make sure:

- Your hands are ahead of the ball. Picture a straight line from left shoulder down the arm and shaft to the clubhead.
- Weight is 70:30 in favour of your front foot.

Move your feet close together for this short swing. Finally, pull your left or front foot back from the target line. It pulls your whole front side back, giving your arms room to swing through to the target.

Rule 2: Let backswing length control distance It's easier to strike the ball cleanly when you speed up through the ball. Acceleration helps you move weight forward through impact, encouraging a purposeful downward strike.

The enemy to acceleration is making a backswing that is too long for the shot you need to play. You'll have to slow the club down to avoid sending the ball too far. When this happens your hands often overtake the clubhead, causing duffs and thins. If in doubt, make a backswing that might be too short and make sure you speed up.

Rule 3: Push through the ball You'll hit more chips on line when you develop the feeling of pushing the clubhead through the ball **(below)** – almost like a footballer playing a side-foot pass. In other words, keep the face of the club looking at the target until the end of the followthrough **(inset)**. Do not allow the face to rotate so that the toe points to the sky.

USE ONE SHOT TO CHIP

If you can be sure of getting down in two most times from just off the green then the vast majority of high and mid handicappers out there will see a dramatic reduction in their scores.

The way to do this is to stop trying to be too clever from the fringe by playing a variety of lofted shots and stick solely to playing the easiest and safest one of all – the putt-chip with a 7- or 8-iron.

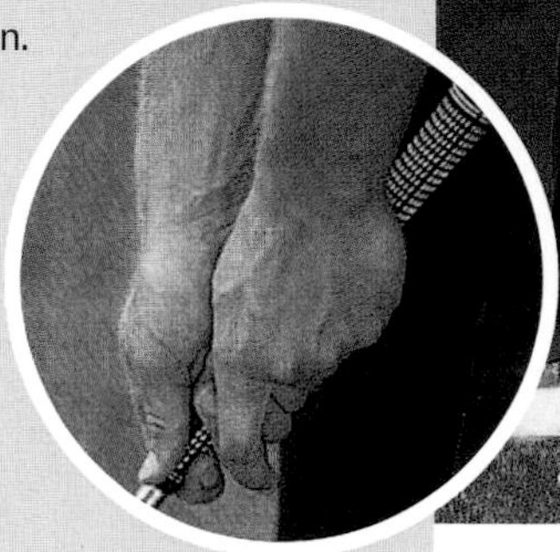

The set-up Stand fairly square to the target line, with the feet close together and your weight slightly favouring the front leg. Position the ball opposite the instep of the back foot, which will automatically place the head and hands in front of it. Grip well down the handle with your normal putting grip **(inset)**.

Playing the shot Having set yourself up correctly, all that's required is a sound putting action, ensuring the clubhead travels back and through low to the ground and your head and hands remain ahead of the ball until after the ball has been struck **(above)**. The angle formed by the wrists at address remains unchanged **(right)**. Because of the position of the ball at address, the strike will be clean and the natural loft on the clubface will lift the ball just off the ground and propel it on to the green with plenty of forward roll. Time spent getting to know the pace required for various distances and conditions will pay big dividends.

IGNORE THE BALL IN THE BUNKER

The bunker shot is the only shot in golf where you don't hit the ball – that's if you don't count air shots! Beginners struggle in sand because they do not have a clear picture of what they are trying to do with the club through impact. Note it well – with the correct bunker technique the club enters the sand behind the ball. The face then pushes sand against the ball as it swings forward, and the ball rises up and out on a cushion of sand.

It follows that you should place your attention on hitting the sand, not the ball. Here are the tools to do just that. Note too that your sand wedge has 56 degrees of loft. Let it do the work for you – you don't have to help the ball out of the bunker.

Step 1: See the sand divot The picture above shows how the club enters the sand a few inches behind the ball and exits after the ball is on its way. Your sand divot should be around six inches long. The ball should be just past halfway in that sand divot, as shown.

This is how it should look to you **(inset)**. You may have heard about aiming your body left and clubface right in bunkers, but forget that for now. Just keep everything square.

Step 2: Play the ball opposite your left heel This is several inches further forward than normal. It puts the point where you want the club to enter the sand (the start of your sand divot) opposite where the ball usually is. This helps you focus on the sand, not the ball.

Step 3: Accelerate through the sand Sand is heavy and brings the club to a standstill unless you are positive with your move through the ball. High handicappers often fail because they can't bring themselves to speed up enough for a shot where the ball is so close to the hole. It takes practice and a bit of courage, but you must swing through briskly to get the club through the sand.

Step 4: Swing to a finish Your followthrough tells all about how well you've been able to speed up through the sand. As a rule you're looking to get your hands to shoulder height. Any lower and you may well find the ball still in the sand.

CONTROL THE SPIN

If you are looking to shoot in the 70s, your target from greenside traps should be to get the ball close enough to have a good chance of holing the putt. To achieve this you need to be able to adjust your technique to suit the shot. You'll need to learn how to play a runner with low backspin when the pin is a long way from you, and to play a high, stopping shot when the pin is cut tight to the trap.

There are two keys to these shots; tempo and swing shape. Here's how to alter these to suit the shot you require. Also, don't go blindly for the sand wedge – give yourself options by using the other lofted clubs in your bag.

LOW SPIN: SLOW AND WIDE
Backswing – Low wrist hinge Taking spin off means a quiet hand action. Begin this on the way back. Keep your hands and wrists as passive as possible. As well as cutting down on spin, this gives your swing a wider arc that promotes a lower ball flight.

Through the ball – Smooth and wide Of course you need to accelerate through the ball with all trap shots, but a lower running shot needs a gradual speed-up with soft hands. Make sure you get your hands to chest height at least through the ball, but do not allow your wrists to flick at the ball. Feel you're hitting the ball forward, not up.

What club? Choose your pitching or gap wedge. Now you are looking for lower spin and a flatter ball flight. These straighter-faced clubs will give you both, while still having enough loft to send the ball out and over the average bunker lip.

HIGH SPIN: FAST AND SHARP

Practice swing – Palm faces the sky The best image is of trying to 'cut the legs off the ball' – in other words, fire the blade through sharply just under the ball. Practise this without the club **(inset)**. Feel as if the leading edge of your right hand is going to cut under the ball as it zips through the impact zone.

Backswing – Loads of wrist hinge You'll find this action easier to make when you bring plenty of wrist hinge into your backswing. Wrist action is what allows you to make that sharp chopping-the-legs-off move through the sand.

Through the ball – Brisk tempo, fast hands The faster you can move your hands through the ball, the more backspin you will generate. So cut those legs off at a pace **(above right)**. Keep your action sharp, crisp and speedy.

What club? Choose your sand or lob wedge. The more loft, the more backspin the face will produce. And of course the ball will fly higher and shorter.

BASE YOUR STRATEGY ON LIP AND LIE

With fairway bunkers it is vital you think your tactics through before taking on the shot. That's because if you fail to factor in two elements – the lie of the ball and the bunker lip in front of you – you can start to look daft very quickly.

You want to get into the habit of being decisive in fairway sand – make a conscious decision on whether to go for the green or to lay up. Here's how to read lip and lie to determine your tactics as well as a great technique for powering the ball to the green and a safety-first plan for advancing the ball a decent distance down the fairway.

Read the lie When the ball is perched clean on the top you can get the clubface cleanly on the back of the ball (see left ball). If the lip's not too high, take on the shot to the green. If the bottom of the ball is below the general sand surface level (see right ball), forget the green. Instead, take a lofted iron and play for position.

Pick the club for the job Of course, sending the ball over the lip of the trap is your priority. Make sure you pick a club with enough loft to do that. If unsure, try standing on the face of the club and looking at the angle of the shaft – it gives a good indication of the height the ball will rise.

Backswing Take the club back wide and low, club almost on the surface of the sand for the first 12 inches or so. Keep wrist action down. This pre-programmes the shallow arc needed for a level, sweeping impact. Remember, keep it wide to let it glide.

Impact Aim to just scrape the top of the sand as you swing through. The club swings forward through impact – not rising or dropping. If you struggle to get this sand-grazing impact, practise without a ball. Swing till the sole brushes the sand.

Set-up From a poor lie you need to hit down to dig the ball out. A simple aid here is to place your attention forward of the ball. So picture a glove in front of the ball; it represents the sand divot you are looking to take. This aids a downward hit.

Impact Squeeze down and forward in the sand. Your aim is to catch ball first, sand second. Forget distance; this is safety first. Use the divide-by-two rule. If you are 180 yards from the green, two blows of 90 yards will do you fine.

GET OUT FROM UNDER THE LIP

How about this for a nightmare scenario? You're under the face of a greenside bunker at a par 3. You try to get the ball out to the hole, but it catches the lip and rebounds on to your foot for a two-stroke penalty. You then chip out backwards out of the bunker, pitch on to the green and take two putts for an embarrassing eight on your card.

Here's how to play this shot properly and give yourself the best chance of getting out on to the green.

Open the clubface Use a really weak grip **(inset)** to open wide the face, and set up for a normal splash shot – body weight should slightly favour the left foot and the ball should be well ahead of centre **(above)**.

The key to success This lies in what you do as the clubhead enters the sand. Make a conscious effort to let the bottom hand 'flip' past the top one **(right)**, throwing the sand and the ball almost vertically upwards – as opposed to the normal forwards and upwards **(top)**. The clubhead also misses the face of the bunker rather than slamming into it.

THE RIGHT CLUB FOR SAND

Playing from sand can be a bit of a daunting task for most mid and high handicappers...and becomes even more so when their equipment is ill-suited to the type of sand they are playing from. Here are the two most common types of sand you can expect to encounter in greenside bunkers and the type of sand wedge that works best from each of them.

MID HANDICAPPER

Light and fluffy This type of sand calls for a club with plenty of bounce (about 12–13 degrees) in the sole to prevent the leading edge digging in too deeply and robbing the clubhead of the necessary speed through impact to get the ball out. The leading edge should be aimed at the target **(right centre)**, but your feet and shoulders should be left of it. Swing along the line of the feet to produce an out-to-in clubhead swing path, allowing the bounce on the sole to do its job.

Heavy or wet The danger here is that the sole will bounce and skid into the middle of the ball, causing it to thud into the face of the bunker or take a low flight through the green. You therefore need a club with minimal bounce. To help the club penetrate the sand, aim the leading edge at the target **(left below)** but stand with your feet and shoulders less open to it than for a shot from fluffy sand. Now take your normal swing and try to make a full, balanced finish.

KEEP IT SIMPLE FROM FAIRWAY BUNKERS

Most 100-shooters know from bitter experience what happens when you get even a few grains of sand between ball and clubface. The sand completely muffles the force from the clubhead and the ball flies like a mince pie, usually settling in the sand a few feet in front of you. So everything you do in fairway traps should be aimed at striking the ball clean, even a little bit thin as long as it clears the bunker's lip.

Here are some straightforward techniques that will pull the bottom of the club away from the surface of the sand and help you make that clean strike. You might start topping the ball at first. That's fine; with practice you can refine your strike to hit the ball pure.

Stand taller The angle of your spine at address plays literally a pivotal role in striking fairway trap shots clean. You should feel that, as you set up to the ball, your spine angle is a touch more upright than normal **(below)**. This will make you feel taller in the sand. This more upright spine gives you two clean-strike benefits; first it pulls the clubhead away from the sand, making it less likely for you to catch sand before ball. Second, it encourages a slightly flatter swing plane – in other words you will end up swinging more around your body than up-and-down. That stops the clubhead ploughing into the bunker and helps you pick the ball off the sand.

Grip tight, grip down Grip firmly, enough to get your knuckles white. That tightness shortens your muscles and restricts your movement, which helps keep your action short and precise – ideal for fairway traps. Also 'shorten' the club by leaving an inch between the grip's butt and the heel of your hand **(inset)**.

Look at the top of the ball Normally you would look at the back of the ball. But a subtle shift to the top just lifts your point of focus and adds another element that will encourage a sandless strike.

Swing as if you were on ice You'll find it easier to achieve the precision this strike needs if you can keep still over the ball. That means minimal weight shift and an armsy swing. Keep your arm swing controlled and your left heel planted.

Work on the feeling of staying still through the ball. Both feet should feel grounded at impact, with leg action kept to a minimum.

Keep this swinging-on-ice feeling to the finish. Keep your feet floored until the end, when your right heel can be pulled up a touch. Let your arms do the work.

DON'T LOOK UP

More short putts are missed by looking up too soon than because of any fundamental faults in alignment or technique. It's all about learning to trust yourself and avoiding the AA – anticipation and anxiety – and staying down on the putt, rather than lifting up to see your success.

✓

Look down Staying down on the putt, eyes steady, allows your putterhead to track through on line, your back shoulder rocking gently towards your chin **(right above)**. This enables the ball to find the line you've chosen for it. Your feel grows with your confidence.

✗

Poor technique Lifting up and out of the putt – usually through anxiety – throws your shoulders **(right)** and your stroke off-line, even with the tiniest peek. Your feel for the putt evaporates as your worry takes root. The only way you'll beat anxiety is by holing more putts – and the only way to do that is to trust your stroke.

MARK THE LINE

It is great to hit towering drives off the tee, but the majority of players would reduce their scores significantly if they holed out a bit better over a round of golf. Here is a very simple tip that you can use while playing, and it should make you hole more putts.

Line your ball Put a straight line on your ball with a marker pen. An arrow will help the image of the ball rolling into the hole.

Aim the putter Having read the break of the putt, simply line the arrow with where you want the ball to begin. And then aim your putter-face perpendicular to the line on the ball.

Easy alignment
Some putters have lines on the top or back of them; this makes it even easier, as you can match the line on the putter to the line on the ball. From here it's simply a matter of rolling the ball end-over-end along the line or arrow and, if you have read the break correctly, the ball will go in the hole.

PUTT WITH TOPSPIN

Ever wondered why your putts hit the edge of the hole and spin out, while on TV pros seem to lip in all the time? The answer is topspin. Pros brush the top half of the ball with an upward stroke, causing the ball to spin vertically end over end. This spin makes the ball want to dive down when it meets any part of the cup.

Sidespin, or even backspin – applied when you hit down on or across the ball – makes the ball spin away when it hits the hole. It's time you hit putts with topspin.

Aim to keep your vertical line upright as the ball rolls.

Mark your ball You'll see how the ball spins by drawing two lines round the ball, at right angles to each other **(left)**. Hit putts with one of the lines you have drawn vertically. When you get the ball rolling with end-over-end topspin **(above)**, the vertical line will look as if it is holding its position.

HOW TO APPLY TOPSPIN

Ball forward Position the ball opposite your left instep **(left top)**. This encourages an impact after the putter's arc has levelled out (around the middle of your stance), when it has begun to rise. This is perfect for that upward strike.

Take it back low You can only hit up on the ball if the putterhead starts forward from a low position, so almost feel you are brushing the grass with the sole of the putter on the way back **(left)**. You'll find this pretty easy if you keep hands and wrists quiet and arms extended.

Scrape the top of the ball In slow motion, practise moving the putter forward and scraping the top of the ball with the bottom of the face **(left below)**. Feel almost like the putter's face is going to clear the top of the ball. Get used to this feeling, as if you are trying to take the paint off the top of the ball.

Refine the movement After you've worked on this upward movement, refine it. Go slightly faster each time, until you can perform your normal-speed stroke while still catching the top half of the ball **(left bottom)**.

GET YOUR ARMS IN LINE

The path of your stroke will follow the line of your forearms. If one sticks out at set-up – as is the case **(right)** with the left forearm creeping out in front of the right – it will throw your putter off-line through the ball. To check this, start by letting your arms hang from your shoulders.

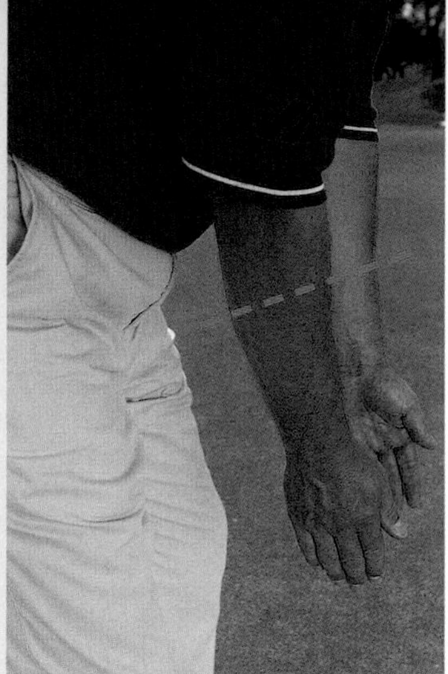

Let it hang Check your forearms are in line, hanging equally far from your thighs.

Arms lead path Your stroke path and the line of the ball follow the line of your forearms.

CUP YOUR FACE TO SEE THE LINE

Even good players can struggle with shorties because they set up with their head at an angle. This puts their eyeline at odds with the ball-to-hole line, which gives them a distorted view of the putt. To beat this, forget your putter for a second and use your hands to cup your face.

Keep it equal When your eyes are square, you'll see equal amounts of both hands.

Cup your face Place your hands against the front of the sides of your face as shown.

TAKE THE GUESSWORK OUT OF SLOPES

Aim to hit the ball one foot further for every foot it has to climb.

One of the areas where high handicappers struggle most is when up against a green with a strong slope they have to putt up or down. This challenge is particularly hard on a strange course. It can be difficult to see past the prospect of a three-putt. There's no magic to dealing with this – just think it through, following these tips.

Add power for uphill putts 'Never up, never in' is never more relevant than when you're faced with an uphill putt. It's so easy to leave an uphill putt short, but there's a simple solution. Just imagine the green is flat and add an extra foot in distance for every foot of the slope your ball has to climb. The steeper the slope, the more distance you'll have to add. Once you've worked out how much further you'll have to hit the ball, walk to the hole and make a mental note of the spot you should now be aiming for.

Putt with caution on downhill slopes An uphill putt can come up painfully short, and a slick downhiller can go racing past the hole. Again, it's easier to picture your green as flat as a pancake and deduct a foot of distance from you to the hole for every foot of slope the ball must travel down. The steeper the slope, the more distance you should deduct. Once you've worked out how much distance you'll have to take off your putt, pace it out from the hole back to your ball and make a mental note of the point you should be hitting to.

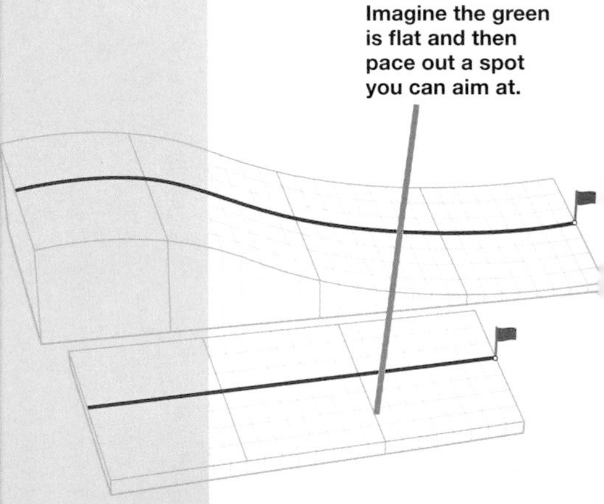

KEEP THE PUTTER LOW TO THE GROUND

Shedloads of shorties are missed because the putter travels in a V-shape, lifting up steeply away from the ground on the way back and then striking down on the ball.
It makes the ball jump off the blade and skip erratically along the ground. Beat it by keeping the putter low to the ground.

Positive putting On short putts many amateurs take the blade back too far and slow down through impact. Result – a nervy waft and a missed putt. Keep your stroke positive by making a short backswing and a firm, accelerating strike.

Balance is crucial Like many things with putting, stance width is pretty personal. But your feet should preferably be almost shoulder width apart. If they are any narrower you run the risk of losing your balance during the stroke.

Line up the logo No doubt you've seen tour pros taking great care to line the ball's logo up with the hole when replacing their ball on the green. This isn't just for pros; lining the logo doesn't just help you see the line, it makes squaring the blade easier too.

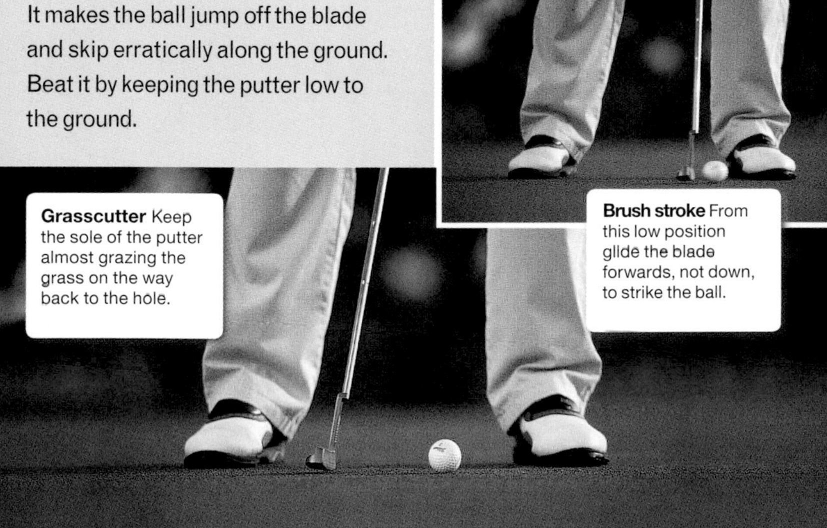

Grasscutter Keep the sole of the putter almost grazing the grass on the way back to the hole.

Brush stroke From this low position glide the blade forwards, not down, to strike the ball.

'TOE' THE QUICK PUTTS

How many times, after two good shots, have you been faced with a fast downhill putt, raced it by the hole and missed the one coming back – scoring an infuriating bogey when a birdie was just reward? Well here's a method to help coax the ball to the hole.

The idea is to create an intentional mis-strike, resulting in a dribbling putt that should wind its way to the hole. As with most shots in golf, the key is in the set-up.

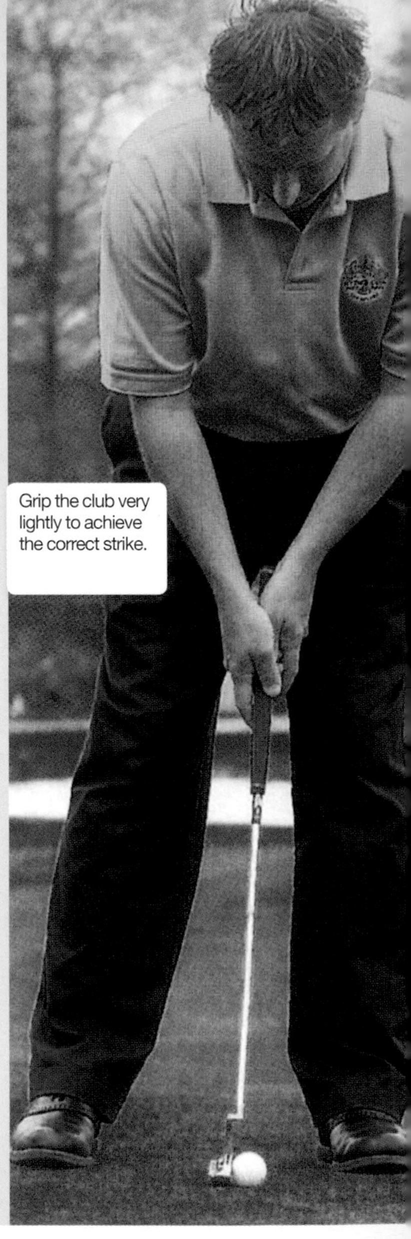

Grip the club very lightly to achieve the correct strike.

Correct set-up Position the ball on the toe-end of the putter **(right)** and then lift the heel of the putter by raising the hands at address. Grip the club lightly, almost to the point where the club will fall out of your hands.

The heel of the putter should be raised and the ball addressed off the toe.

Successful mis-strike The result of the off-centre hit **(above)** and a light grip is a dull strike that has little forward momentum and is therefore guaranteed not to speed past the hole **(left)**.

PART II: ON-COURSE STRATEGY

A TIGHT DRIVE

It's a long par 4 with a narrow fairway. You need accuracy and length, so bite off as much as you can chew.

HIGH HANDICAPPER

The play You must play away from the worst trouble – in this case, the canyon left – so aim well away, up the right, and make some adjustments to stop the ball cutting into trouble.

The club Use a lofted wood, perhaps a 5-wood, or a utility club if you have one. It's the best compromise of control and power.

NO RISKS
Pick a line well clear of trouble – even drive the ball on the safe side of that line.

STRONG GRIP

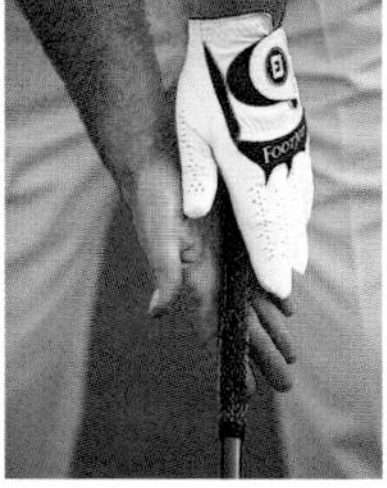

Position the top palm mainly on top of the grip and the lower palm mostly below it. This is known as a strong grip. It will help you to rotate the clubface to a square or slightly closed position through impact, preventing the slice that could send your ball tree-ward.

SORT SHOULDER AIM

Your shoulders have a big say in controlling the swing path, so make sure they're aiming where you want the ball to start – in this case towards those trees on the right (but short of them). Place a club across your chest to see where your shoulders are aiming.

HIT TO 1.30

Your one swing-thought is to drive the ball to the right, away from that canyon. Make this easier by picturing a clockface holeside of the ball, with 12 o'clock your target line. Hit the ball to 1.30 (right of your target). You'll start the ball in play and promote a draw.

MID HANDICAPPER

The play The ideal ball flight will follow the shape of the hole. That means starting right, then bending gently to the left. So set up to hit a soft draw. It's not as hard as you think.
The club Use a 3-wood. The face has more loft than a driver and offers a little more forgiveness, but it is still straight enough to apply plenty of sidespin.

MID HANDICAPPER

SHOULDERS SHUT

At set-up, develop the feeling you are looking slightly over your left shoulder. This will place your shoulders in a slightly closed position, promoting an inside path for your backswing. This will help you to attack the ball from the inside, leading to a draw.

BUTTONS BEHIND BALL

As you swing down, keep your centre line – represented by your shirt buttons – behind the ball. This calms your downswing and stops you lunging forwards, causing a choppy slice. It also sets up a wide, sweeping move through the ball, which you'll need for a draw.

SEE GLOVED FINGERS

To move the ball right to left you must rotate the clubface through impact, which means rolling the right forearm over the left. Your forearms should practically be touching, the right on top. You should also be able to see the gloved fingers of your higher hand.

RIGHT SHAPE
Swing smoothly to the safe side of the hole. Turn your forearms to produce a draw.

CLUB TO LEFT KNEE

Angle your spine away from the target to get a sweeping angle of attack and place weight behind the ball. Here's how to find the right angle: hold the club against your chest, shaft on your centre line. Now drop your back shoulder until the butt nudges your left knee.

LEAN AWAY

To make this powerful position at the top of your backswing, you must move off the ball into your right side. Find this 'leant-away' position at the top, preserving the spine angle you set at address. From here you have space to move into as you start your downswing.

RIGHT SHOULDER LOW

Develop the sensation that your right shoulder is moving below and past your chin as you swing through. Anxiety will tend to make you straighten up through the shot. Once you lose your spine angle, you'll probably lose the ball too – usually way right.

BE POSITIVE
Commit to the shot. If you ease up through the ball you'll lose timing and line.

LOW HANDICAPPER

The play Despite the tight fairway, this is a longish hole and you don't have a shot here, so you need to get up in two. Play a positive shot to the safer side of the hole.
The club Take a driver. Although modern drivers hit the ball with low spin, you should feel comfortable drawing on your most powerful club.

PAR 3

Do you miss the green on par 3s all the time? If so, just change your tee-up position.

Par 3s offer a birdie opportunity for all golfers, no matter what their handicap. These holes are set up to reward accuracy, so any advantage that big hitters have is lost. Hit the green and you've a guaranteed birdie chance. Sounds simple, doesn't it!

But let's face it, most golfers miss more greens than they hit. To make life a little easier, you must learn to work with your natural shot shape, to ensure you have the best chance of finding the putting surface. If you slice the ball left-to-right, then the right side of the tee is your best friend. If you hook the ball right-to-left, the left side of the tee is your best option.

If you still miss, here are three ways to make up-and-down to save par.

MID HANDICAPPER

The hooker
The trouble down the left side of this hole is a big threat to your shape shot, so tee up on the far left of the tee and aim at the right-hand side of the green. This gives room for the ball to move from right to left in the air, landing on the green.

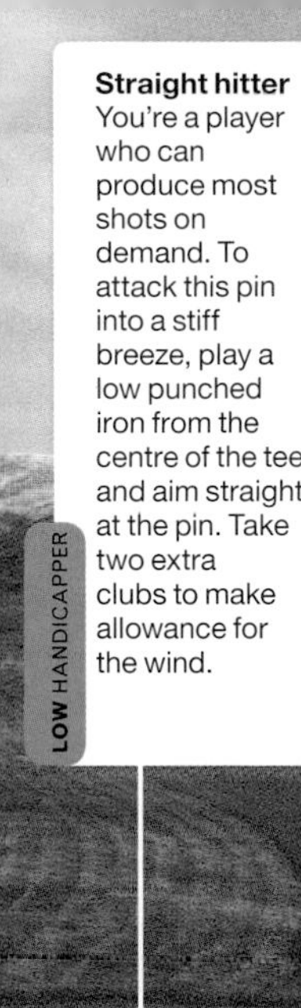

LOW HANDICAPPER

Straight hitter You're a player who can produce most shots on demand. To attack this pin into a stiff breeze, play a low punched iron from the centre of the tee and aim straight at the pin. Take two extra clubs to make allowance for the wind.

PAY ATTENTION TO THE PIN
When you're faced with a tough tee shot, you really have to pay attention to the pin position when you're lining up on the tee. The pin here is tucked on the far right side. Your best option is to play a fade in from the left to attack it. Always look for slopes up ahead on the green as well.

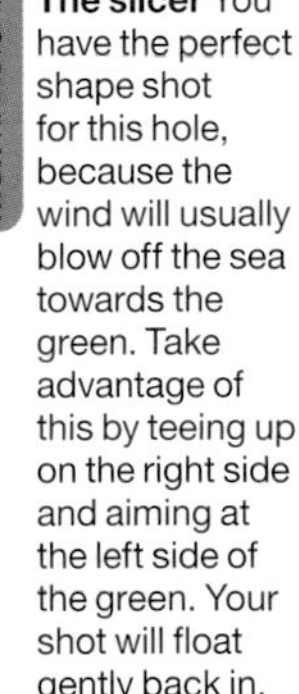

HIGH HANDICAPPER

The slicer You have the perfect shape shot for this hole, because the wind will usually blow off the sea towards the green. Take advantage of this by teeing up on the right side and aiming at the left side of the green. Your shot will float gently back in.

GET UP-AND-DOWN
Your tee shot has failed and you've missed the green. You could easily destroy your scorecard by racking up a big score, with a poorly played recovery shot. Use your short game skills to save your par.

HIGH HANDICAPPER

TEXAS WEDGE It is almost impossible to land a chip on to this vicious downhill slope with control, so using a putter to get the ball rolling down the slope is your best bet. Remember to read the slopes of the bank as you would a putt. Aim right to allow for the big swing back down to the pin. Always lean with the slope, not against it, and make sure your eyes are directly over the ball so you see the line.

MID HANDICAPPER

PAR 3

ROUGH RECOVERY **Your ball is sitting down in deep rough just off the edge of the green.** The upslope will add loft to the club, so use a 9-iron rather than a pitching wedge.

Play the ball forward a touch in your stance...

and make sure your swing follows the steep angle of the slope.

LOW HANDICAPPER

POT BUNKER SHOT **Blasting out of a monster pot bunker is no easy feat.**

You need to open your sand wedge wide and lay it flat before gripping.

Set up with your hands slightly behind the ball at address, keeping maximum loft as the club sweeps through the sand.

200 YARDS OUT

...and a ditch in front of the green, what do you do? Here are strategies and techniques for all levels.

HIGH HANDICAPPER

The play Hit two shots of 100 yards with a 9-iron or pitching wedge. Your chances of hitting the green in one are slim, so take the trauma out of this tough shot by using the 'divide-by-two' rule . Hit two short shots, well within your capability. You can even use the first one as a practice shot for the important one into the green.

DIVIDE BY TWO
Hit two 9-irons to the first green. Use the first as a dry run for the second shot.

SET-UP

Play the ball just back of centre. You want to make a short, crisp swing that takes a neat divot. This ball position – a little further back than normal – encourages a downward strike on to the ball. Also narrow your stance a touch – it promotes a shorter swing.

BACKSWING

Swing back until your hands are no higher than your head. You may be 200 yards from safety but this shot is not a quest for distance. Hopefully, with a 9-iron in your hands, you'll abandon any thoughts of distance. Think balance and control.

DOWNSWING

Aim to finish your swing in this position, with weight on your front foot and back toe. Your hands need reach no higher than your chin. This shot is all about precision, seeing how well you can split this 200-yarder into two controlled pitches.

MID HANDICAPPER

The play Your mission is to strike a fairway wood over the hazard to the green. For a mid handicapper, this is the percentage shot. You should be able to clear the ditch at the front, and the fairway wood gives you a chance of hitting and holding the green. Even if you miss, you should have a fairly straightforward up-and-down.

MID HANDICAPPER

THE TECHNIQUE

It is essential to keep the same spine angle from set-up to the top of the backswing. It's equally important to retain that angle through to impact, especially with fairway woods. The low loft on these clubs mean you need a steady, sweeping arc to strike the ball well; you can only find that arc from a consistent body pivot, your spine angle staying the same through the swing. Place a club against the small of your back **(above left)** and practise turning back and through, the shaft and spine angle staying as constant as possible **(above centre)**.

WATCH FOR THIS

It's so easy to straighten up through the ball. It usually happens because you are trying to hit the ball too hard. With your body pivot lost, you'll almost certainly top the ball along the ground. To avoid this, keep your backside stuck out as you swing through the ball.

HAVE A CRACK
Take on the shot with a fairway wood. Keep your height constant for a good strike.

LOW HANDICAPPER

The play Hit a fading long iron into the green. The left-to-right fade will help you get the height and soft landing you need to hold the green. It's not the easiest of shots but if you aspire to break 80 it's a shot you should be able to pull off. Use a 3- or 4-iron, depending on wind, slopes and, of course, your power.

3-IRON FADE
This shot gives you the best chance of hitting and holding the green.

SET-UP

Pre-programme your fade by aiming feet, hips and shoulders 10 yards left of the pin (right for left-handers). Your swing path follows your body aim. This makes it easier for you to start the ball left, the first essential ingredient of a fade.

BACKSWING

Keep the clubhead 'outside' your hands. As you swing back, feel for the sensation that, with the shaft parallel to the ground, the clubhead has not flicked back behind your hands. This sets you up for a slightly outside-the-line backswing, which is perfect for a soft fade.

DOWNSWING

Pull left through the ball. It ensures your body keeps turning and leads your hands to the hitting zone. With hands trailing, the clubface stays open to your swing path and applies cutspin to the ball. If your body stops, your hands take over and roll the face shut.

IN THE ROUGH

Make the sensible choice out of deep grass and avoid a scorecard disaster.

All golfers go a little offline from time to time – some more often than others! The difference between good players and the average club golfer is that they know how to recover from these tough lies. Rather than delve into the bag for a long iron or utility wood, the sensible player picks out their wedge or a lofted iron and knocks the ball back into play.

There are the odd occasions, however, when going for the pin is a viable option. Take the example shown here: only 120 yards from the green, and a simple pitching wedge would get there under normal circumstances. But do you dare take on the shot?

Here are three options for you to consider – and yes, one of them is going for the green. But remember, you must be 100 per cent confident to attempt a do-or-die shot.

HIGH HANDICAPPER

There's no point messing about. Look for your easiest and safest route back to the fairway and get the ball back into play. The nearest point of relief is out to the right, and from here you'll be left with a simple pitch up on to the green.

IN THE ROUGH

HIGH HANDICAPPER

Playing out of tangly rough, you simply can't predict how the ball is going to fly. The club can turn over very easily, so what's the point in risking leaving it in the rough? The most sensible play is to find your safest route back to the fairway and get the ball out.

HIGH HANDICAPPER

You'll need your most lofted club to drive your ball out of deep grass. A lob wedge is good, but a sand wedge would also work. Make sure that you take a full swing and drive down powerfully into the back of the ball. If you quit, the ball won't come out.

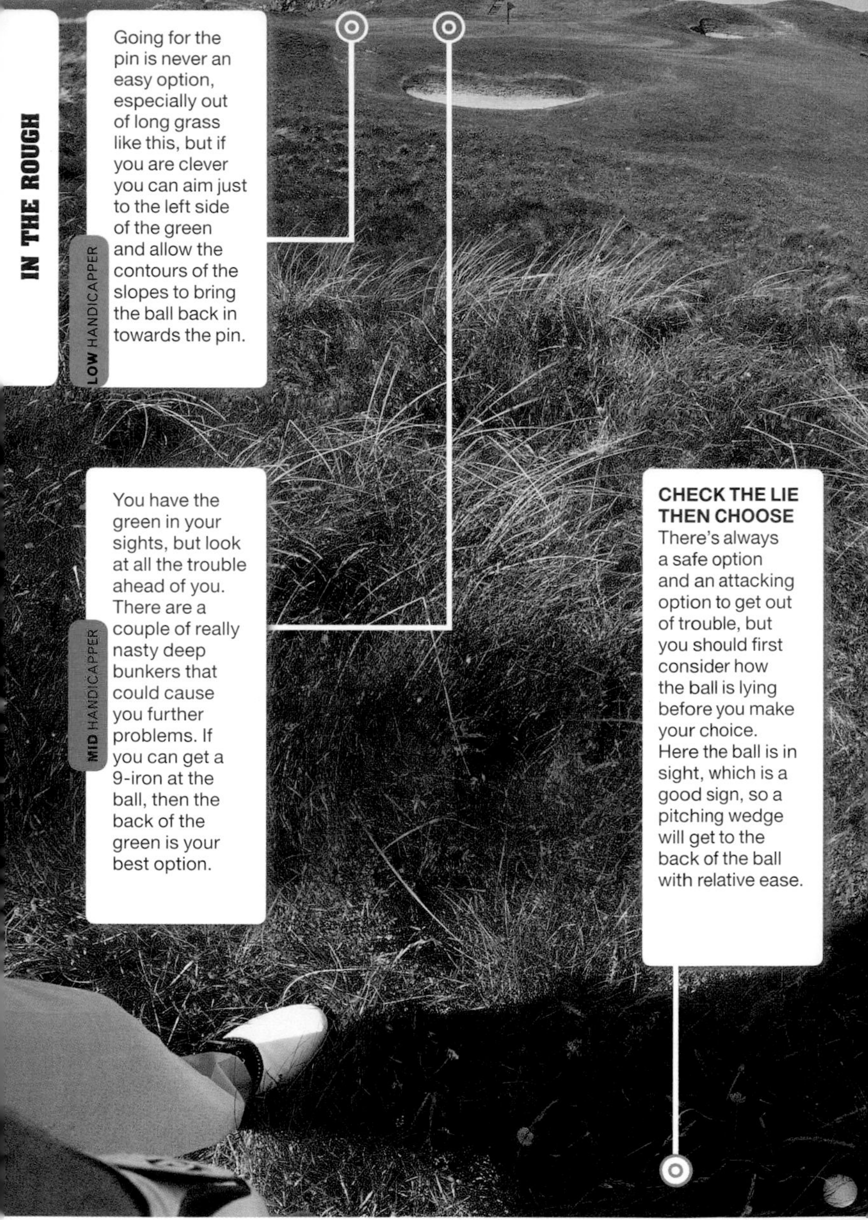

LOW HANDICAPPER

Going for the pin is never an easy option, especially out of long grass like this, but if you are clever you can aim just to the left side of the green and allow the contours of the slopes to bring the ball back in towards the pin.

MID HANDICAPPER

You have the green in your sights, but look at all the trouble ahead of you. There are a couple of really nasty deep bunkers that could cause you further problems. If you can get a 9-iron at the ball, then the back of the green is your best option.

CHECK THE LIE THEN CHOOSE

There's always a safe option and an attacking option to get out of trouble, but you should first consider how the ball is lying before you make your choice. Here the ball is in sight, which is a good sign, so a pitching wedge will get to the back of the ball with relative ease.

BACK OF THE GREEN You have the skill to hit your ball all the way to the back of the green, so here are a couple of small adjustments to make sure it comes out.

Grip down and grip tighter to stop the clubhead twisting in the grass.

Drive down steeply into the back of the ball for it to pop out.

THE ATTACKING PLAY If you want to save par from this tough spot, you'll have to learn to keep the arms connected to the upper body as you swing through.

The butt of the club should be opposite the chest as you swing down.

The hands lead the club, and keep your glove facing forward.

IN THE FAIRWAY BUNKER

Get yourself out of this tricky predicament.

HIGH HANDICAPPER

The play Forget the green. A high handicapper should simply aim to get the ball close enough to the green for a simple pitch. Just knock it up the fairway some 100 yards.

The club Use a 9-iron. The face has enough loft to clear any fairway bunker lip, and for the shot you're going to play – almost like a fairway punch shot – this is the ideal choice.

GET DOWN
Try to hit down on the ball, so you strike it ahead of sand.

HIGH HANDICAPPER

BALL BACK

Play the ball just behind the centre of your stance. Add a little weight to your front foot (perhaps 60/40). You may feel your right knee kick in a touch. Check you have virtually a straight line from left shoulder to clubhead. These measures promote a downward hit.

GET STEEP

Don't be afraid to make a fairly sharp backswing, the club rising quickly from the sand. Increase the effect by leaving some weight on your front foot. Keep it short and controlled, with your left arm maybe just past parallel with the sand.

BALL FIRST

Everything you've done so far has been to build a descending angle of attack, the club swooping on the back of the ball. This is to avoid catching sand before ball, and thereby muffling the shot. The downward blow means that the club carries on down into the sand after making impact.

SHORTEN THE CLUB

Hold your 6-iron an inch further down the grip. At once you feel like you have more control of the clubface – and that hitting sand before ball would need an almightly downward lunge. Keep the ball position central to help you make that clean strike.

HANDS TO EAR HEIGHT

Although you're playing this shot much like a fairway strike, the fact you're on sand means your foundations are less stable and you need to be more precise with the strike. Use a three-quarter backswing and you'll swing with more stability and control.

LEVEL KNEES

You need to make a forward-swinging level hit, taking only a thin scrape of sand. Keeping knee caps level, or feeling like your belt is horizontal, are both excellent swing thoughts. They'll help you construct the stable base needed for this shallow hit.

SHORT GAME
Swing within yourself to boost your stability and the accuracy of your strike.

MID HANDICAPPER

The play The percentage plan here is to play a clean three-quarter shot that ends up short of trouble near the green, but close enough for a shortish pitch and putt.

The club Play something like a 6-iron, or any club that will get you 140–150 yards up the fairway. A 6-iron should also have plenty of loft for you to clear the trap lip.

GO FOR IT
Use a utility wood and play to hit to the wide side of the green.

LOW HANDICAPPER

The play Low handicappers should have the ball-striking ability to go for the green. Play to the open side of the green.

The club If you don't own a lofted utility wood, get one – if only for this shot. You can hit down on it like an iron and the ball still rises. The flat sole helps the club skid where a 3-iron might dig.

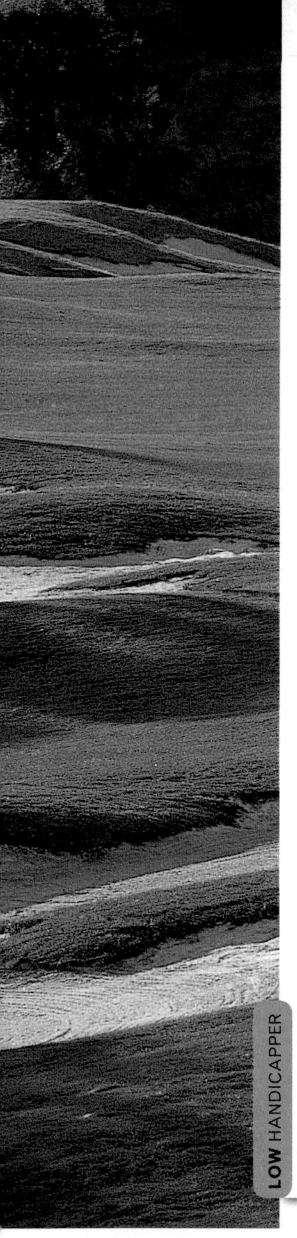

BALL FORWARD

Position the ball midway between your left instep and the middle of your stance. This spot, around the low point of your swing arc, offers the best combination of clean striking, while letting you use the full loft on the clubface. Hold the club half an inch down the grip.

QUIET CHANGE

Where this shot is most likely to go wrong is at the change of direction. You're 200 yards out in sand, and it's tempting to lash the ball. Start down no faster than you ended the backswing – a calm change of direction – and trust rhythm and timing to find the distance.

PHOTO FINISH

Programme this finish into your swing. If you know you're going to finish in perfect poise, it has a really positive knock-on effect on how hard you swing at the ball. Keep your through-swing relaxed and full, and you'll play this shot with the confidence of a pro.

IRON TO THE GREEN

It's easy to get greedy with your approach shot. Choose the sensible play.

HIGH HANDICAPPER

The play There's trouble on the right, so a simple shot to the front left of the green is your safest option.

The club Use one or two clubs more than you'd pick for the yardage and play a three-quarter shot for optimum control and accuracy.

PUNCH IT IN
A lower ball flight is more controllable, so keep the swing short and hit left.

HIGH HANDICAPPER

AIM LEFT FOR SAFETY

Your line here is the front left quarter of the green, or where the high bank finishes and the green begins. Pick a spot on the ground ahead of you, which runs straight to this point, and use this as an alignment aid to help you set up squarely. Aim your body left.

CLUB UP

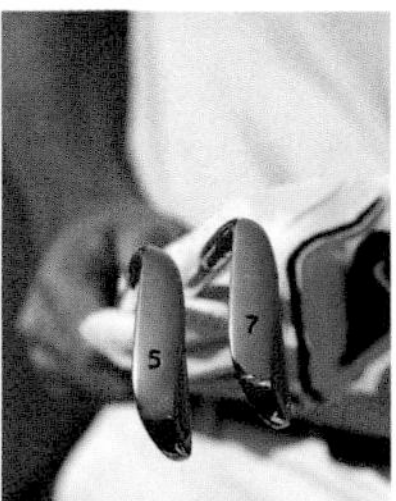

You are 150 yards out – the temptation is to take the least lofted club you need to get there. Actually, by taking an extra club and swinging easily, there is a far greater chance you'll strike the ball straight at the target, rather than slicing it into trouble.

SHORTER SWING

A short swing is a controlled swing, so make sure your backswing is no longer than three-quarter length. Keep thls abbreviated swing for your followthrough and your approach should be razor straight. You could also grip down the shaft a little, for even more control.

TAKE DEAD AIM

If you want to be more aggressive then you need to be 100 per cent sure you are aiming where you want to go – the centre of the green. Hold your club up and use its shaft as a guide, and use it to pick a spot of ground ahead with which you can align yourself.

BALL GOES BACK

To make sure you send your ball soaring on a lower trajectory, simply put the ball position back an inch or two in your stance. This will de-loft the club and encourage you to make a more descending blow into the back of the ball, launching it on a lower flight.

RELEASE THROUGH

Shot shape is key here. The ideal is a right-to-left shape that will take the water on the right out of play. To do so you'll need to put draw spin on the ball, and by rolling the wrists (turning them over) through impact you will impart the desired spin.

SAFELY DOES IT
Aiming for the centre of the green is a sure-fire way of making your par.

MID HANDICAPPER

The play A sub-90 shooter can be a little more aggressive with their approach. Aiming for the centre of the green is the best play, as it allows a little margin for error while being attacking enough to leave you with a long birdie putt.

The club Again, it would be wise to use a little more club than you'd naturally select and swing easy if you want to be accurate. One more club than the yardage suggests should be sufficient, and you should try to punch the ball on a lower trajectory.

SHARP SHOOTER
Be aggressive with your approach and home in on that tricky pin.

LOW HANDICAPPER

The play Set up to hit a slight fade, starting the ball at the left side of the green and allowing it to move back towards the pin before landing.

The club Take an extra club. A fade (left to right) will naturally come up a little shorter than the equivalent straight shot.

BALL GOES FORWARD

By pushing the ball position forward an inch or two in your stance, the club will return to the ball on a more upward, and slightly open, path. This will open your body alignment and encourage the fade (left to right) spin and will also give a higher, softer-landing ball flight.

SPINE ANGLE BACK

Tilting your spine back a touch at set-up (so your head is just behind the ball) will help you to swing upwards into the air. This will give you a much higher ball flight, and the ball will land softly with control, to help you attack the pin far more easily.

EXTEND AND TURN

The key to playing a successful fade shot is to ensure your clubface remains a touch open as you strike the ball. Stretch and extend your arms as far as possible away from your body, on a slightly outside path, as you swing back.

OBSCURED BY TREES

There's more than one way back to the fairway after a slice into the trees. Pick the shot to suit your game.

HIGH HANDICAPPER

The play Forget that gap up front between the trees or, even worse, thoughts of a high exit. Just reach into the bag for a club with more than enough loft to simply knock the ball out sideways, via the easiest route, back on to the fairway.

BE POSITIVE
Watch your swing and stay down, in order to get a clean ball contact.

BALL BACK IN STANCE

The pitching wedge has more than enough clubface loft to do the job. Check at address that the ball is positioned a little further back than normal, to help make sure the clubhead doesn't get tangled in the grass before reaching it.

SAME LENGTH

The danger with this shot is quitting at impact. Concentrating on keeping the lengths of the backswing and through-swing the same will help you to eliminate the chances of a duffed shot, and result in an overall smooth and crisp action.

CHEST FOCAL POINT

Coming up on the shot with a flicking action through impact is another common mistake, and always leads to disaster. A good way to stay down through and beyond the hitting zone is to 'focus' your chest on the ball.

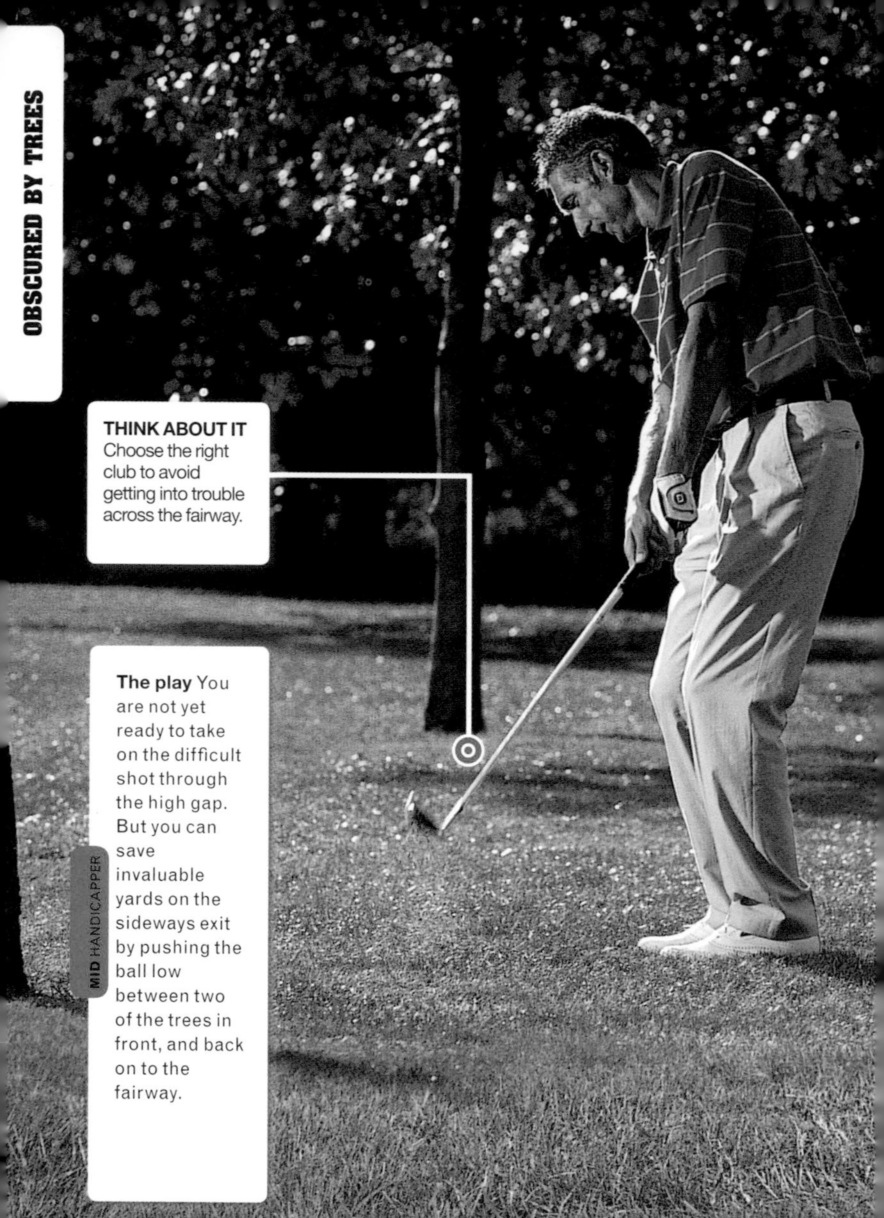

THINK ABOUT IT
Choose the right club to avoid getting into trouble across the fairway.

MID HANDICAPPER

The play You are not yet ready to take on the difficult shot through the high gap. But you can save invaluable yards on the sideways exit by pushing the ball low between two of the trees in front, and back on to the fairway.

KEEP IT SAFE

It's easy to apply all your thoughts to getting the ball away from the trees, rather than exactly where to play it to. Take time to see exactly how much fairway you have to play with, rather than charging the ball right across it and into more trouble.

CAREFUL CLUBBING

Don't rush your club selection – this needs careful consideration. In this particular case, a 6-iron has more than enough loft to remove the ball from the fairly short rough, but not too much to send it clattering into the branches.

IT'S A ROLL-OVER!

Make sure the clubface is showing its correct loft and is not shut when you sit it behind the ball at address. Then concentrate on rolling your right wrist over the left through the hitting zone, for a crisp strike and low flight under the woodwork.

LOW HANDICAPPER

The play There's no reason why, with careful planning and the correct set-up, you shouldn't attempt to fly the ball through the gap in the top of the trees and leave it within reasonable chipping distance of the pin.

FIX YOUR FLIGHT

Don't take chances. There's no room for the slightest doubt in your mind that you can pull off the shot. Look carefully at how the ball is lying and the trajectory needed to fly it clear of the branches. Have a good mental picture of the shot.

SET-UP

Once you are confident you've selected the right club for the job, set up with the ball forward of centre to get maximum loft from the clubface. With the right shoulder below the height of the left, you need to actually feel you are going to fly the ball high.

FINISH HIGH

Whatever happens, don't be tempted to try to give the ball a helping hand into the air. Just apply all your concentration to driving and accelerating the clubhead powerfully through the hitting zone, finishing high and nicely balanced.

PITCH ACROSS THE POND

There's no green to work with and a river right in front. How good you are dictates what you should do next.

HIGH HANDICAPPER

The play Take a wedge and play safe – aim for the centre of the green. Many 100-shooters have the wrong idea here. A ditch has to be carried and a green has to be held, so they often try to hit a very high shot. It usually means a scooping action that causes duffs and thins. Instead, picture a level hit that sends the ball forwards.

ON THE LEVEL
High handicappers should hit forwards, not up. Let the loft on the club sort the ball height.

HIGH HANDICAPPER

SET-UP

Stand with your shirt buttons level with the ball. That places the ball pretty central in your stance.This ball position – coupled with a subtle weight shift on to your forward side – will help you make the forward hit you need for a solid strike on this short shot.

STAGE IMPACT

Rehearse your impact position just before you take the club away. Place the club on the ground three inches ahead of the ball. Also, allow your shirt buttons to drift forward of the ball. This lets you know how that level strike through impact should feel.

SWING

Hit forwards.
Build two thoughts into your action: first, work on the feeling that you are trying to hit the ball as low as possible. That task will help you find the moves you need for the level, forward hit. Second, try to find that post-impact position you have just rehearsed.

SET-UP

Aim feet, hips and shoulders five yards left of the flag (right-handers). Your swing path will naturally follow your shoulder line; by aiming shoulders left you pre-set an out-to-in swing that cuts gently across the ball, applying soft-landing fadespin to the ball.

BACKSWING

Play this shot with a punchy, purposeful swing, the clubhead zipping across the ball from out-to-in and loading the ball with spin. Give your swing a short-to-long feeling to find this technique. Swing back to hip height only, with no excessive wrist movement.

FOLLOWTHROUGH

Accelerate briskly for the followthrough. Give your swing enough impetus to send your hands through to shoulder height. This will give the ball sufficient power to get to the pin, as well as packing the ball with cutspin for a soft bounce.

FADE AWAY
Cut across the ball to apply fadespin to hold the ball within 15 feet.

MID HANDICAPPER

The play Mid handicappers should be looking to get up-and-down. That means pitching to around 15 feet or closer. To get the ball that close you're going to need to generate a little extra height and some cutspin, which helps the ball settle down quickly on landing. Play a sand wedge and cut across the ball slightly from out-to-in.

TOTAL CONTROL
Play a smooth cut-up shot that gives a high flight and soft landing.

LOW HANDICAPPER

The play From 60 yards, nurture a down-in-two mentality. You are looking to save par from here, or perhaps make birdie on a par 5. An up-and-down means being able to lob the ball inside eight feet from the cup, which calls for a cut-up shot with stacks of spin to hold the ball close to its landing spot. Play a 56-degree sand wedge or 60-degree lobber. Aim left and cut the ball up into the air.

SET-UP

Aim feet, hips and shoulders 10 yards left of the flag (right-handers). This paves the way for the fairly severe out-to-in swing path you need for a cut-up shot. But make sure you keep the clubface aiming at the pin. It will appear open to you as you look down.

SWING

Make a full, one-paced swing for this zero acceleration shot. This isn't a shot that needs power; it needs control, so cut out any speed surge through the downswing. Keep your hands soft, and let the club drop from the top **(above centre)**. This smooth action quietens the shot and gives the ball a soft landing.

Wipe the mud off. Picture the cut-across move you need through the ball by imagining you have mud on the sole of your sand wedge. How would you use the grass to wipe it off? You'd drag the sole along the turf, at right angles to the clubface aim. Bring this dragging action into the shot **(above right)**.

THE LONG BUNKER SHOT

...also known as the hardest shot in golf – apart from the hole-in-one. Pick the technique to suit your standard.

HIGH HANDICAPPER

The play Treat this shot like a chip-and-run. Play a brisk, firm-wristed shot that nips the ball off the top of the sand and sends it skipping to the green.

The club Of course you need enough loft to clear the lip – that's the priority – but pick a weapon that gives you as much help with distance as possible. An 8-iron is normally a good choice.

HIT CLEAN
Keep your body still and wrists firm. Pop the ball like a chip-and-run shot.

HIGH HANDICAPPER

BALL BACK

Position the ball behind your shirt buttons and just inside your back heel. This position will take some loft off the clubface – so make sure you allow for that – but it does pre-programme the downward strike that helps you hit ball first and sand second.

FIRM WRISTS

Increase your grip pressure slightly. It immobilizes your wrists, simplifying your movement. If you're not over-confident, it's the percentage move; calm down your wrist action and you may lose finesse – but you'll ditch a variable that can lead to heavy shots.

STILL BODY

Keep your body as still as possible. Nipping the ball cleanly needs serious precision. The shot you're playing lets you get the ball moving towards the green, even with a slight duff. Help your chances of a clean strike by keeping your body passive through impact.

MID HANDICAPPER

The play Picture a shot that flies mid-height, neither high and floating nor low and running. This is the trajectory you want. It will carry the ball to the front of the green and chase it up to the stick.

The club Take a pitching wedge. It offers the right combination of power and loft – enough to get you over most lips, but with a bit of forward force.

BRUSH STROKE
Use a wedge. Introduce a little wrist hinge to help you hit a mid-height shot to the green.

AIM LEFT

You'll have more success with this shot if you play it as a gentle cut. Holding the face open – or at least square – through impact guarantees you keeping loft on the face. So aim your body just a touch left of parallel to your ball-to-target line.

MORE HAND ACTION

Wrist action gives you more finesse and a greater opportunity to add controlled spin to the shot. But it also creates angles that need to be restored. On this shot, allow for a little wrist play but limit it. You add some feel without making life too difficult for yourself.

TAKE A LITTLE SAND

Hit the sand just behind the ball. Any more and the ball won't go far enough; any less is tough to control with the wrist action you've introduced. Nobody's saying this is easy – but after even a few practice shots your ability and confidence will grow.

HIGH FLIER
Commit to the shot and find a high flight by making a full followthrough.

LOW HANDICAPPER

The play Get the ball close by taking fairway slopes out of play. Hit a high ball that carries to the pin, loaded with backspin to help it settle.

The club Use a sand wedge. Make a fullish swing to generate the speed to load the ball with backspin; it also gives you a high, dropping flight that means the ball won't chase forward.

OPEN THE FACE

Open the clubface just a few degrees. It adds loft to the face, giving you a helping hand in finding that high, soft-landing ball flight. It also just makes the sole of your sand wedge a little more rounded and bouncy, limiting the likelihood of a heavy, chunky strike.

FULL HINGE

Play this shot with plenty of finesse, using your hands and wrists to fizz the clubhead through the sand just under the ball. Keep your hands soft and let your wrists hinge fully as the club reaches the top. From here they can release positively into impact.

BIG FOLLOW THROUGH

You're taking a smidge of sand with the ball, which will muffle impact, so you will only get the ball back to the pin with a committed swing. Your followthrough length indicates that. Let's see your hands by your left ear and shaft touching the back of your neck.

BUNKER IN THE WAY

Popping the ball up and over a bunker on to the green is a tough shot to execute, even for skilled players.

The obvious choice is to grab your sand wedge and try to flip the ball over the trap, but there's a high element of risk in this technique.

There are, however, a couple of alternatives that will get the ball over the hazard. They won't necessarily stop the ball quickly on the green, to land it next to the pin, but they should leave you close enough to have a putt to save par – and that's far better than duffing your shot straight into the bunker and facing an even tougher up-and-down from there.

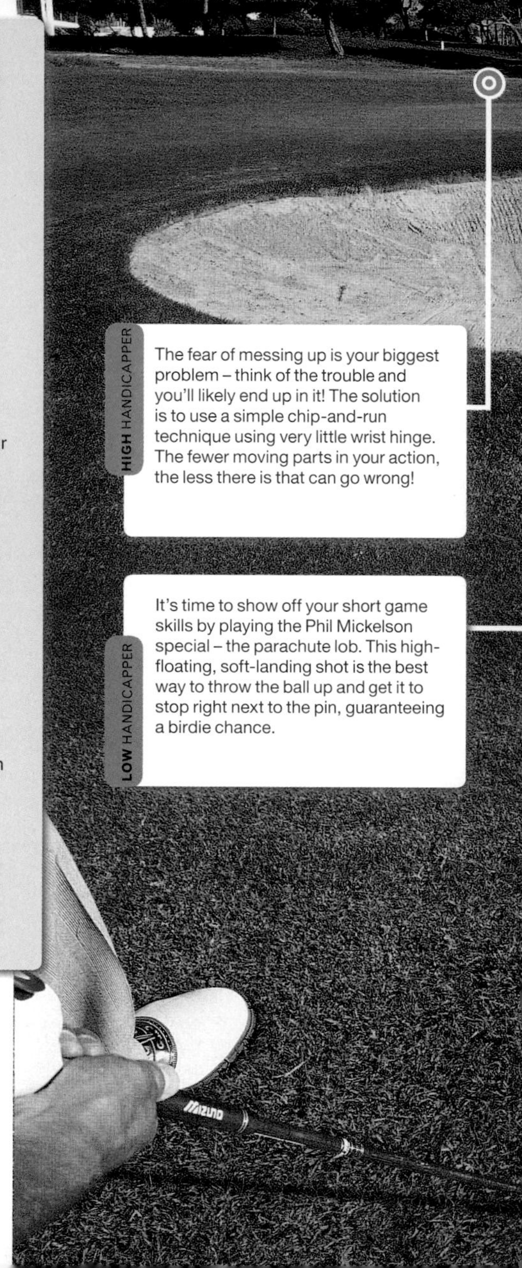

HIGH HANDICAPPER

The fear of messing up is your biggest problem – think of the trouble and you'll likely end up in it! The solution is to use a simple chip-and-run technique using very little wrist hinge. The fewer moving parts in your action, the less there is that can go wrong!

LOW HANDICAPPER

It's time to show off your short game skills by playing the Phil Mickelson special – the parachute lob. This high-floating, soft-landing shot is the best way to throw the ball up and get it to stop right next to the pin, guaranteeing a birdie chance.

MID HANDICAPPER

You are skilled enough to be thinking of making up-and-down. However, the do-or-die parachute lob carries a lot of risk. Use a simple chip technique with an open stance. Your ball should pop up and over the trap and land with a little run out.

CHIP IT FORWARDS
As you chip the shot forwards, make sure your hands stay ahead of the clubface. Doing so will keep maximum loft on the club, ensuring the ball pops up and over the sand before running out.

HIGH HANDICAPPER

SAFETY FIRST

This is the sort of shot you frequently mess up, but there is a simple solution. Just use a chip-and-run technique. Set up with the ball positioned towards the back of your stance and keep your hands forward of the ball. Your weight should favour the left side, and keep it there throughout the swing.

MID HANDICAPPER

SURE-FIRE CHIP Position the ball in the centre of your stance, keeping your hands level with the ball and your weight forward.

Aim left, but keep the clubface square to the target.

Make a short backswing and through-swing. The ball will pop up higher than a normal chip and will run out less.

LOW HANDICAPPER

POP AND STOP Lay the club wide open and take your grip.

Your hands should be a touch behind the ball, with the grip pointing at the zip on your trousers.

Exaggerate your knee flex and make a full, soft swing with plenty of wrist hinge. Let the club overtake the hands to flop the shot up high.

IN THE GREENSIDE TRAP

It's easy to get too clever from the bunker and end up in a right mess. Get it right and get it out.

HIGH HANDICAPPER

The play Down in three is always a good result from any bunker. So base your strategy on giving yourself a putt for your next shot. If the pin is tucked, forget it and hit positively to the part of the green that gives you the most margin for error.

The club Use a sand wedge for a normal shot. If the lip is especially steep you could use a lob wedge.

SAFETY FIRST
Take the safest option, even if that means hitting away from the pin.

HIGH HANDICAPPER

IN THE GREENSIDE TRAP

HOVER THE CLUB

Ideally, the sole of your sand wedge will hit the sand two inches or so behind the ball and plough on through. The club never hits the ball – it forces sand against it, which lifts it out of the bunker. So begin by hovering the sole above the contact point on the ball.

SHAFT AT SKY

On short sand shots it feels all wrong to make a full swing. But a half swing makes you tentative. So hit the sand firmly – it will always deaden impact – and make at least a three-quarter backswing. Picture the shaft vertical, with the clubhead pointing to the clouds.

SHOW YOUR SPIKES

If you do quit on the shot it will happen on the way down. Your right side will resist rotating purposefully through the ball. Get over this by moving off that back heel and showing your spikes to anyone behind you. It forces your right side to rotate.

AIM A LITTLE LEFT

This short shot can trick you into thinking you need all sorts of craft and handwork to cut the ball up. Forget all that. Your best strategy is to hit past the pin, which means treating this like a standard splash shot. Aim a couple of yards left for a gentle cut.

FOLLOW THE FOOTLINE

A common error is to open your stance, only to pull the club back inside as if following a line to the hole. This puts your swing path at odds with your alignment and leads to mishits. Let the clubhead trace a line parallel to your toes – it keeps your swing on track.

HANDS PAST LEFT EAR

As you swing, a part of your brain will try to convince you to slow down and hit softly – after all, the pin is only 10 feet away. But any deceleration could see the club stalling in the sand. Ignore that voice and swing crisply to a fullish finish, hands travelling past your left ear.

KEEP IT SIMPLE
Don't try too hard. Hit past the pin, leaving a makeable putt coming back.

MID HANDICAPPER

The play Getting out of the bunker will only be a problem for you if you try to get too clever, so play past the pin. Aim for a point 10 feet or so long to leave yourself a fighting chance of a par.

The club Both sand or lob wedge is fine, but if the sand is thick and heavy go for the extra weight of a sand iron.

GLANCING BLOW
Aim left and cut across the ball. Use the length of followthrough to control distance.

The play Even with little green to work with, the 70-shooter should possess the clubface control to land the ball between the edge of the green and the pin. So play an attacking shot for a simple up-and-down.

The club Use a lob wedge. The extra few degrees of loft on the face will help you to find the steep, yet soft, trajectory this shot needs.

AIM WAY LEFT

The further left you aim, the more of a glancing blow you'll get (the clubface is open to this swing path). This means only a fraction of the club's force is sending the ball down the line to the pin, allowing you to keep swinging with purpose on this delicate shot.

LONG WAY BACK

Keep your backswing full and rhythmic. This shot needs ultimate club control coming into impact, with virtually zero acceleration; if your backswing is short you will be tempted to hurry the club through. Get your hands up around head height.

SHORT SHIFT

Swing down with minimum force. Feel like you're going to let the sand slow the clubhead down and shorten the followthrough. On a really short shot, the clubhead shouldn't get much above knee height. This takes some practice – but it's a great technique to master.

FRIED EGG IN THE BUNKER

You're faced with a 'fried egg' lie in sand and you don't know how to splash the ball out. Here are three ways to recover from this nightmare situation.

HIGH HANDICAPPER

SAFELY DOES IT

When you reach the ball, check to see how close your ball has plugged to the lip. If it's under the lip then look at the ground to the sides of the bunker and aim to play out to the side that offers the best chance of a two-putt.

CLOSE THE CLUBFACE

Turn the toe of the club inwards and then take your grip. You should still hover the club behind the back of the ball, but aim to hit down steeply into the sand. By closing the clubface the club will drive down far easier into the sand.

PICK CLUB UP STEEPLY

Your backswing should be short and steep. Use plenty of wrist hinge to raise the club up, so that it points straight up at the sky. From here, you just need to drive the clubhead down into the sand. Be positive, don't quit on the shot and the ball will pop out.

KEEP IT SIMPLE
Don't be too ambitious, even if that means hitting out sideways.

HIGH HANDICAPPER

The play The only thought that should go through your mind is to get the ball out, by whatever means possible. Look for the nearest route back into play – if that means hitting sideways, then so be it.

The club Use your most lofted club – either a sand wedge or a lob wedge – but make sure you close the clubface, because you'll be hitting down into the sand.

TAKE AIM
By hitting into the widest part of the green you will make a two-putt more likely.

MID HANDICAPPER

The play Attacking the pin is not really the sensible option for you. Instead, look for the widest part of the green and aim to splash the ball out to this point, hopefully leaving yourself in two-putt territory.

The club A sand wedge is the only option if you are going to attempt to play forwards over the lip. Make sure the clubface is square, as the natural loft will do the work for you.

THE SENSIBLE PLAY

Don't get greedy and try to play for the pin. The sensible play is to aim for the widest part of the green, because the lip of the bunker you'll have to carry is less steep and you'll have a greater margin for error. You can still two-putt for par from here.

SQUARE THE CLUB

You don't need to open or close the clubface at address to play this shot effectively. The natural loft on your sand wedge will do all the work for you. Simply concentrate on hitting the sand just behind the ball as you would for a normal shot in sand.

SHORT IS BETTER

The nature of this shot means you'll be taking a lot of sand in order to get the ball out, and as a result your followthrough will be stunted. Don't worry if you don't reach a full finish position; just ensure the club drives beneath the ball, enabling it to pop up and out.

ALL OR NOTHING
This difficult shot requires a club with lots of loft, and a hard hit into the sand.

The play This is a really specialist technique that should only be attempted if you have a high skill level out of sand. You'll be aiming straight at the pin, and hitting down hard and fast into the sand, then allowing the club to immediately recoil back towards you.

The club You definitely need plenty of loft on your club to play this shot, so a sand wedge – or even better a lob wedge – is essential.

GO FOR THE PIN

The power that goes into this shot should mean the ball pops out no matter what direction you hit it in. It may seem bold but aiming straight for the pin is definitely the right move, because you'll give yourself the best chance of getting up-and-down.

OPEN THE CLUB

You need maximum loft on your wedge to play this shot well, so open the clubface as wide as possible before you take your grip. Then hover the club a few inches behind the ball, at the point where you want it to enter the sand.

HIT AND RECOIL

The harder you can hit down into the sand, the better, because as soon as you hit it you should feel the club recoiling back towards you. This makes the club bounce through the sand, so helping the ball to pop up high and land softly on the green.

A RIDGE BEFORE THE GREEN

With only 10 yards to the hole... and a ridge in the way, what shot should you play? Let your ability decide.

HIGH HANDICAPPER

IDENTICAL PRACTICE

Get into the habit of making at least two practice strokes. With each, focus on making it a complete dry run for the real thing. Make the rhythm and length of the stroke as near to what you'll need as possible. It makes executing the stroke much simpler.

BACKSTROKE – SOFT WRIST

Let your wrists hinge a little as you reach the end of your backswing, your left wrist flattening and the back of your right wrist flexing. Wrist hinge is a force source, and even a small move like this can load some extra firepower into the putterhead.

THROUGHSTROKE

Maintain your spine angle. Even well after the ball is on its way, avoid the tendency to straighten up. Just having the intention of keeping your spine angle will stop you lifting up and out of the putt – a move that kills your strike quality.

STAY DOWN
Stay bent over the ball till it's well on its way to the hole. Lift up and you'll mishit the putt.

HIGH HANDICAPPER

The play Your percentage shot is to keep the ball as low to the ground as possible and run the ball over the ridge.

The club As long as the grass is no longer than fairway length, take a putter. It takes a lot of the risk out of the shot – no chance of duffing and thinning, and no poor kicks to worry about.

TURF HUGGER
On this chip shot, keep the clubhead low and to the ground and take it back through.

MID HANDICAPPER

The play Use the ridge. Aim to land the ball on top – there's a reasonable margin for error here – and let it trickle down the other side to the pin. This shot takes out the chance of the ball snagging up on the longer grass.

The club Take an 8-iron or something close to it. This loft is enough to send the ball over the longer grass but not sufficient to carry the ball on to the downslope or the green. It also has enough power to help the ball run up the slope if you underhit it.

SET-UP

Get your head over the ball. Don't set up as you would for a full shot; get in close, with your hands down the grip and your feet close together. Positioning your head over the ball helps you see the line; it also makes it easier to move the club up and down the line.

BACKSWING

The two big errors on this shot are trying to scoop the ball in the air and stabbing the ball down. Both can cause fats and thins. Beat both by aiming for a level hit, the clubhead staying low to the ground. Picture your hands running along a horizontal shaft.

FOLLOWTHROUGH

Use this thought: 'Keep a constant gap between your elbows.' Do this and you can't fail to keep your hands quiet through the stroke, boosting your chances of striking the ball cleanly. Any change in your elbow gap is a certain sign of overactive hands.

SET-UP

To execute this bump-and-stop shot you need to give the ball a crisp downward blow. Alter your set-up to make the job easier. Play the ball opposite your rear instep. Sit your hands forward of the ball. Keep a straight line between left shoulder and clubface.

HEAD OUTSIDE HANDS

Don't let your wrists work the club back in behind your right hip on the way back; they shouldn't be releasing the club on the way through either. Run the face almost straight back and through from its set-up position, with minimal in-to-in movement.

FACE LOOKS AT TARGET

This shot is played firmly, but with virtually dead wrists. Resist the tendency for the face to fan open on the way back or rotate shut on the way through. As an intention, aim to keep the clubface looking at the hole from start to finish.

FACE TO TARGET
Boost accuracy by keeping the face outside your hands back and through.

LOW HANDICAPPER

The play Hit a bump-and-stop shot that takes the ridge completely out of play. You're looking to hit a firm shot with a lofted club that flies the ridge, pitches on the green then – with the help of a little backspin – settles down quickly on the second or third bounce.

The club Take a wedge or sand wedge, which offers 52–56 degrees of loft. That's enough to clear the bank and apply plenty of backspin to the ball, helping it sit down on the green.

THE TEACHING PROS

Gareth Benson
Teaching professional at the Astley Golf Range, Manchester

Jason Brant
Head professional at East Berkshire Golf Club

Chris Brown
Head professional at Westin Turnberry Golf Resort, Ayrshire

Gary Casey
Head coach at Thorpe Wood Europro Golf Centre, Peterborough

Nick Clemens
Head of Advertising at Provision Golf, Isle of Wight (formerly a teaching professional)

Alistair Davies
Senior teaching professional at The Belfry, West Midlands

Andrew Etherington
Former teaching professional at The Belfry, West Midlands

Jason Froggatt
Head teaching professional at Four Seasons Resort, Al Badia, Dubai

Adrian Fryer
Head teaching professional at Drivetime range, Warrington

Craig Jacoby
Former teaching professional at Silvermere South East Academy of Golf, Surrey

Nicky Lawrenson
Teaching professional at the Emirates Golf Club, Dubai

Stuart Morgan
Former head teaching professional at The Grove, Hertfordshire

Mark Reed
Director of coaching at Machynys Peninsula Golf Club, Carmarthernshire

Lee Scarbrow
Head teaching professional at John O'Gaunt Golf Club, Bedfordhire

Derek Simpson
Senior teaching professional at The Belfry, West Midlands

Simon Wordsworth
Former head teaching professional at The Belfry, West Midlands